Poker Strategy

POKER STRATEGY

Winning with Game Theory

NESMITH C. ANKENY

Basic Books, Inc., Publishers

NEW YORK

Library of Congress Cataloging in Publication Data

Ankeny, Nesmith C
Poker strategy.

Includes index.
I. Poker. 2. Game theory. I. Title.
GV1251.A54   795.41'2   80–68177
ISBN: 0–465–05839–6

CONTENTS

Contents

LIST OF TABLES

ACKNOWLEDGMENTS

I would like to acknowledge the valuable assistance of Robert N. Ross in the preparation of the manuscript for this book. I am also indebted to Jim Simons for his mathematical collaboration twenty years ago when these poker ideas were first preoccupying me.

I am particularly and fondly grateful to my grandmother, Edna E. Ankeny, who first taught me to play cards and win.

Of course my primary tutors have been my poker-playing friends. My special gratitude is to Bernie, Lou, Marshall, Mert, Nick, Norm, Ozzie, Persi, Berl, Pat, and Roger.

PREFACE

Never play poker with a man called Doc.
Never eat in a restaurant called Mom's.
Never sleep with a woman who's got more troubles than you.

NELSON ALGREN

What is this book about, and why should any reader trust the advice it offers?

This book tells you how to play poker, winning poker. There are four attributes required to become a skillful poker player, or, indeed, to be a winner in almost any game from old maid to chess: technical ability, discipline, judgment, and hustle. These virtuous qualities are interrelated and can be acquired with effort. Now let us examine these qualities and see if my advice can be trusted.

Technical ability translates into knowing what hands are sufficiently strong to open and what hands qualify for a call, a raise, or possibly a reraise. It also includes the ability to mystify your opponents so that they are never sure whether you have a power house or a bluff hand, to rationally interpret other players' bets, and to understand the dynamics of poker.

Discipline is the ability to control your own actions and to keep your own emotions from interfering with your technical skill. This includes being able to concentrate, to note and to remember all the information around the table—an obvious attribute but one that is often difficult to maintain when losing or playing against obnoxious opponents. Certainly discipline is as desirable in any game from tennis to polo.

Judgment can be translated into experience, alertness, and elementary gamesmanship. It is needed in the few rare but important times when technical skill is not enough. When an opponent makes an exotic play and the interpretation is cloudy, chaos and disaster seem to lurk. Here experience and understanding the principles and ideas behind the technical play help. Here a true expert will come up with a very bold, or possibly an ultra-cautious, play.

Hustle is a player's ability to guard against anything from a flagrant lack of courtesy to outright cheating—anything from needling a loser to peeking at another player's cards. I'm certainly not advocating such activities, but a player must be able to protect himself from such lamentable but ubiquitous human behavior.

Of these qualities necessary to develop into a good player, the emphasis in this book, and in my opinion the most important, is on technical skills. For example, discipline is not of critical importance when a player doesn't know what is the correct play. Also, I have seen games where known cheats were tolerated because they were such poor technical players that they lost their money as well as their integrity. Thus, the emphasis will be on technical skills in poker. Fortunately, a poker player needs only an ability to reason, whereas in tennis a good player also needs coordination and in polo he needs a clever horse. Later in the book, especially in the last chapter, we shall return to the other qualities I have listed, but not before we have mastered technical abilities, so critical to the playing of poker. Then, possibly, the reader will trust my advice.

The reasoning and rules presented in this book require a minimum amount of simple mathematics. They can be easily understood by the eager and motivated poker player, who, having mastered the book, will understand the basic play and can go on to win at poker.

CHAPTER 1

Introduction

Poker is the science of deception. Scientific poker allows the player to choose a rational course of action much as a point-count allows a bridge player to decide on a reasonable bid. Bridge players have the advantage here, of course, because generations of players have already devised bidding systems that rationally simplify decision making in that complex game.

Poker strategy is still in its infancy. Perhaps people have not taken poker seriously enough to study the theory of the game; perhaps people have been blinded by the apparent predominance of luck. Whatever the reasons, enough fortunes have been made and lost in the game to warrant at least a serious attempt at understanding the underlying logic of the game and, on the basis of that understanding, framing rules for the best possible play.

The Goal of the Book: Optimal Strategy

The first goal of the book is to be a simple guide; the second goal is to explain the *optimal strategy* (we will define it in chapter 3) by which a player is guaranteed to win at least a certain amount of money and at the same time is assured of losing no more than a certain amount. Optimal strategy is a concept drawn from Game Theory, a branch of mathematics that has proved valuable in many different fields, from the elaborate games of economics and political science to such honest-to-god games as poker.

As a mathematician, I certainly have the credentials to talk about Game Theory, but what can I say about poker? Will the advice given in this book be practical and useful, or will it only be the finespun theory of a mathematician? I can only say that I have found my discovery of the optimal strategy to be a real poker windfall and that I have played according to its rules for the past ten years. My opponents at countless poker tables know best whether the strategy works or not.

I strongly believe that understanding the reasoning behind the strategy will make you a better player. It will also give you a much keener intellectual enjoyment of the game. If you simply want to play better poker and are not especially interested in the theoretical underpinnings of the game, taking the rules as gospel will satisfy your needs. But if you would also like to know more about Game Theory itself, you will find this book an exciting and rewarding application of that theory to the actual game of poker.

An important part of a betting strategy is the almost auto-

4

matic, built-in deception, usually called a *bluff.* This built-in deception applies not only to betting but to other aspects of the game. In draw poker, for instance, the number of cards a player draws should be determined by a consistent pattern of deception that gives no aid to the opposition. The optimal strategy is the proper balance of deception and strength yielding the maximum guaranteeable profit over the long run.

The Myth of Luck

The worst enemy of the poker player is luck—not good luck or bad, but the concept of luck itself. A poker player considering luck in planning his moves at the poker table is like the Pope contemplating marriage. The thought is heresy and can only lead to trouble. The goal of a poker strategy is to minimize the effects of luck.

Let me give you an example. The game was Jacks-or-better draw poker. Player A opened with a pair of Aces; Player B called with a pair of 6s. Player A caught a third Ace in the draw; Player B came up with four 6s. The betting was heavy and Player B won a large pot, but why did he even try for the pot with such a small pair in the first place? He said that he felt "lucky" and that somehow the cards "knew" his lucky feelings and were generous to him. Player B was living in a fool's paradise. His cards had no sympathy for his or anyone else's feelings. By the end of the evening, Player B came out a loser and was a consistent loser in the following sessions. He finally gave up poker and now talks about luck to his bowling partners.

Forget about luck. The worst thing that could happen to a young man on his first encounter with a slot machine is for him to win the jackpot. That slot machines are bad investments for everyone but the owner is obvious, but try to convince the "lucky" young man who desperately tries to duplicate his winnings. He eventually throws back many times his original jackpot and probably never continues his "lucky" start. On the other hand, the young man who initially loses a few hard-earned dollars on the slot machine may realize that this is not a good investment. In the long run he is far better off. Any thought about luck is poker blasphemy. Let us waste no more time on such evil.

The excitement of the game stems from the uncertainty and deception that thread through an evening of poker. Cards have neither memory nor conscience, but most of the uncertainty in poker comes from the cards. This book deals with how to tame these uncertainties. But it might well pay to give a little thought to the human beings who will be sitting at the table with you.

The Role of Psychology

Because poker is a game played by people, many observers of the game claim that successful poker players have learned to handle people and know how to read the most subtle signs of their intentions. Possibly, but only possibly, there is something to this. If a player makes a big bet without hesitation or bets and then lights up a cigarette, it may well have great significance, but only a spouse or a psychiatrist can know with any degree of certainty what the gesture signifies. In the end, the significance may have nothing to do with poker. I have long given up trying to figure out what the significance might be. It is far more profitable to ignore such gestures, because for our limited purposes they are irrelevant. Of course there are consistently "tight" or "loose" players with whom you might vary your tactics, but the best way to learn to play good poker is to assume that each opponent is an expert player and that personal idiosyncrasies are beyond your ken.

The player at the table to whom you can most profitably apply some elementary psychology is yourself. Psychology at poker can be reduced to this simple most important rule: Keep your own emotions under control; they should not cloud your judgment. The nature of a poker game makes discipline a difficult task. But if you cannot discipline yourself, poker is not the game for you.

Guidelines

Before we get down to particulars of the optimal strategy, a few practical guidelines will help dispel popular myths about poker.

Play only for stakes you can afford. Only you can know

what stakes you should play. If you feel the game is over your head, stop playing. On the other hand, if you can afford the entertainment of a good poker game, risk your money. Some people spend more on liquor than they do on groceries. Cadillac owners often make less money than Volkswagon owners. There is nothing wrong with a person spending his money on what he enjoys. I have met millionaires who will only play in small limit games, and I know a poor graduate student who will play in any game if it doesn't cost more than a couple of thousand to sit in.

The decision is yours. If you think the game is too much for you, get out. Nothing is easier to spot than the fear of a player who feels he is financially over his head. His play deteriorates, and his opponents will chew him up.

Poker is the most pleasant way to gamble that I know. It is neither necessary nor desirable to turn a poker game into Russian roulette to make it fun. Any poker game is interesting as long as the players take the game seriously and play intelligently. To insure that players take the game seriously, stakes must be "reasonable." They must be high enough to add spice to the game but not so steep that a loser is driven to desperation. In some of the examples in this book, I specify the amount of the pot or the bets. I use sums that are reasonably significant, but I don't mean to frighten you or to influence the sums you play for.

The 20/40 ante rule. In a table-stakes draw-poker game buy enough chips so that you have at least twenty times the ante. (At stud try to have a least forty times the total ante.) For example, in a seven-man draw-poker game, where each player antes 50 cents and the total ante is $3.50, I would recommend having at least $70 worth of chips in front of you before each hand. Keep enough money in your pocket so that you can replenish your stack if necessary. If you start losing and you have only $40 in front of you, buy another $30 worth of chips. Don't wait until you're wiped out before buying more chips.

Advance spending limit. Try to set a limit, in advance, on the amount that you are willing to lose in a game. If you reach this limit, make a tactical retreat. Curse the winners if you wish, but go home. There is a tendency in all of us to buy another $10 worth of chips, just to see if our luck will change. This action only prolongs the agonies of losing. It makes no sense to keep playing without sufficient chips to make (or call) a couple of raises should the situation demand it.

Importance of position. The seating arrangement at the table is as important in a poker game as the gate position in a horse race. There is nothing mystical about its importance. Strategic seating, (and I don't mean a "lucky chair,") can give a player a concrete edge over all other players. You can play your position with respect to the other players.

Here are some of the most important considerations: (1) If there is a conservative player in the game, try to get a seat to his left, immediately to his left if possible. When this conservative player is betting or raising you will have advance notice and can get out of his way. (2) Conversely, try to get to the right of a wild player, or at least halfway across the table from him. A wild bettor is liable to drag down several players, usually the players to his left. When playing against a wild man, try to be in a position to pick off his bluffs without too many players remaining behind you who can benefit from the action by sandbagging (passing on big hands and waiting for "sport" to whoop up the betting).

There are other nuances with respect to position that

might well depend on how the game is going. If a strong player changes his seat, it might be profitable to give some thought to his action.

Sometimes there are purely technical considerations. I played in a five-card stud game in Las Vegas where the casino furnished a "house dealer" who sat at the table, not to play poker, but to take care of the dealing for which he "cut the pot" for the casino. The house rule was that the player with the high card on the first round was forced to make the first bet. If there were two or more players with the same high up-card, the player to the left of the dealer was faced with a mandatory bet. If you have a deuce in the hole, a mandatory bet is compulsory philanthropy regardless of how high the up-card may be. It is now evident that the player immediately to the right of the dealer—that is, farthest to the left —has a considerable edge: Namely, he can quietly fold his weak hand. Without a house dealer and with each player dealing in turn, no seat enjoys this permanent advantage.

When to leave. "The winners tell jokes, and the losers cry, 'deal.'" This truism describes the irrational and counter productive conduct that any student of human behavior will find at the poker table. A winner must have been doing something right and should want to continue playing. A loser should want to adjourn the game and wait for a more fortuitous time. The question is often not whether a player will lose but how much. Having lost both his chips and his detachment, the loser is in the worst possible position to go on with the game.

Human nature and variations being what they are, it would be unrealistic for me to give advice on when to quit a poker game. And I might not follow my own advice, however solid. But it might be of help to give some consideration to your own quitting time as an integral part of an overall strategy.

What about cheating? "A gentleman is a man who will pay his gambling debts even when he knows he has been cheated," Tolstoy is reputed to have said.

Two types of poker games should be avoided: a hook game and a crooked game. In a hook game, the casino takes a certain percentage of every pot, ostensibly to reimburse the casino for overhead. Most Las Vegas games are hook games, the house cut varying from 5 to 15 percent. There is nothing necessarily crooked or illegal about such a game, it is just too big an obstacle for a player to overcome. It is like playing with a handicap. The casino "wins" far more than the usual big winner. When playing in a public game, choose one in which the house charge is a fixed fee with no "cuts." The most reasonable clubs charge an hourly fee that varies according to the size of the game. You can easily judge if this fee is out of line.

Crooked poker games are glorified in fiction and ballads and are the topic of much poker gossip. The gossip is probably not completely false, just grossly exaggerated. Players are often accused of cheating but seldom to their faces; the vast majority of such claims, at least when I have been present, usually turn out to be false. Anyone can buy chips; it is far easier to yell thief than to admit to being a miserable player.

Unfortunately, some crooked games exist, but usually they have a telltale odor about them. Something is wrong; exactly what is wrong or who is emitting the fumes is sometimes hard to tell. It is far easier and cheaper to start yawning, claim a bad day, and get out of there than to solve the mystery of who is doing what.

If something fishy is going on in your own home game,

remedial steps can be taken. These precautions are a good idea in a big game, just to avoid suspicion. For instance, when the dealer is through shuffling, he passes the cards to the player on his right; this player makes two or three quick shuffles and lets a third player cut the deck before the deal. Periodically, after the hand is over, count the remaining cards in the deck to make sure that you are playing with a full deck. This only takes a few seconds and is worth the effort.

The real cheating danger is collusion. A five-card stud game or any high-low game can be an absolute paradise for collusion. When two or more players gang up, they can rack up even the best opponents. Also, there is no incriminating evidence. The few gestures on which the collusion is based can be deciphered only after some time has passed, and even this evidence could be interpreted in various ways. However, if the odor of a cheat is there, stop inviting the suspects, or never invite more than one. If they are guilty the message will be clear enough.

Seven Playing Rules

Here are a few simple technical rules that will immediately improve your game. These seven simple rules are derived from my long experience at the poker table and from the scientific method of poker described in this book. The rest of this book will be an expansion and application of these seven rules of good poker, rules that are generally valid and easy to remember. They are designed for Jacks-or-better draw poker but apply equally well for anything-opens draw poker.

1. Do not call the opener with any pair less than Kings. Subsequent callers need at least a pair of Aces (see chapter 2 for the precise refinements).

2. Do not make a first round call with a four straight. There is an old saw about not drawing to an "inside straight," but the sad truth is that an open-ended four straight pull is also a losing proposition.

3. Never draw two cards. Draw one card to trips and (usually) draw three cards to a pair. False carding in the draw is an art, but the skill is knowing when to draw one card, three cards, or to stand pat (see chapter 4 for the refinements).

4. Do not make a first-round raise on two pair. Treat two pair with the delicacy afforded a Ming vase. Two pair are usually strong enough for a first-round call but too fragile to club your opponents into submission by a first-round raise. (See chapter 2 for the strategy on how to call an opponent while holding either two pair or a select number of four flushes to gain the maximum profit from the hand. See chapter 5 for a discussion of first-round raises).

5. Raise on the first round with trips. If the pot has been opened, don't let a hand like trips wilt on the vine by a mere call. By calling you are allowing the opener to improve his hand on the draw without cost (to draw out on you), and permitting other players to sneak in behind you with four flushes, both costly mistakes. (To guarantee the maximum profit from trips, the intricacies of a first-round bluff-raise should be mastered. See chapter 5.)

6. Have a firm second-round calling rule, a rule that depends on the strength of your hand. (For example: Call a bettor only with Queens-up or better.) Without a firm rule a whimsical player is often quite predictable—a seemingly contradictory statement, but not in poker. For example, a big loser will usually make desperate calls, calls on very weak hands, in an attempt to get even. Or toward the end of an evening a small winner will usually tighten up on his calls, not wanting to lose that winning euphoria. Good players can spot this and profit.

7. Be very cautious about overcalling on the second round. If one opponent makes a bet and another opponent calls, you need a strong hand to overcall—a hand that would have justified your initiating a bet if the previous players had all passed to you.

Chapter 2 will explain the basic play of draw poker and, with the aid of some calculations of probability, will give rules for selecting the best opening and calling strategies.

Chapter 3 is a departure from the natural sequence of the game. Instead of immediately presenting basic second-round procedures, the chapter investigates bluffing. Bluffing coupled with high-hand betting is basic to my theory of scientific poker. To understand bluffing is to understand the optimal strategy of poker. By using the example of the opener versus the four flush, we clearly see which hands qualify as bluff hands and which hands qualify as high-betting hands. The concept of an optimal strategy in poker is thus developed and provides the cornerstone for all second-round betting and first-round raising.

Chapter 4 is a return to the natural sequence of the game and provides useful and concrete rules for a basic second-round poker strategy. Having used the specific example in chapter 3 of the opener versus the four flush, I now present the most general case of the opener versus the one caller.

Having mastered chapters 3 and 4, the reader is presented the first-round raising strategy in chapter 5. This optimal strategy is carried through the first and second rounds of betting. The defense strategy is also presented. Chapter 6 presents the theory for three or more players in the second round of betting.

Problems presented at the end of chapters 4 and 5 develop real understanding of the theory behind each chapter. Chapter 7 consists of advanced problems to challenge a poker player's expertise. While these problems arise in actual poker games, they present draw poker at its trickiest; they put the competent mastery of the optimal strategy to a rigorous test. Chapter 7 also shows how the optimal strategy can be modified for certain variations in draw poker.

To win at poker, a player needs technical expertise and practice. This book is about technique. The practice is up to the reader.

CHAPTER 2

Draw Poker: Basic First-Round Play

I have played draw poker in a dingy pool hall in Butte, Montana, where the miners had been out on strike for six months and there was as much action as at a 100-yard dash for snails. I have also played in a private room in a posh London club where there were so many mirrors on the ceiling and walls that I was forced to look at my cards without lifting them from the table. I have played in many settings with many different people, but in all of these games the basic rules and tactics of poker remain the same. The etiquette and the stakes may vary but a flush always beats a straight.

Every poker game has certain ground rules that can vary considerably from game to game. Not to acquaint yourself with all the details may be quite costly. This is not the place for me to go into the esoteric subtleties of some rules governing draw poker. Instead I would like to mention the major common elements that define the game, whether you play in London or Hong Kong.

This chapter gives explicit rules for all first-round opening and calling, always in the context of the position of a player.

Draw Poker: Rules and Definitions

A draw-poker game usually has from five to eight players; seven is the best number. There are not enough cards for more than eight players, and it is not usually a very interesting game for four or fewer.

The game of draw poker consists of a round of betting, a draw, and a second round of betting. It would be hard to find another interesting game of such simplicity.

Before any player receives cards, every player puts up a set amount of money, called the *ante*. If there are six players in the game and the ante is $1, the total ante is $6. The ante is the only blind bet in poker. The whole game of poker after that bet is a fight over the ante, the total ante.

After the ante is paid, every player is dealt five cards called a *hand*. The hands are all ordered as shown in table 2.1.

Starting with the player to the left of the dealer and proceeding in turn to the next player to the left, a player may open or pass. To *open* means a player makes a bet, putting his bet in the pot. In most cases the opening bet should be the size of the total ante. A *pass* means that a player makes no bet. If all of the players pass, there is no winner, the cards are thrown into the center of the table, and the player to the left of the dealer becomes the dealer for the next game. Depending on table rules, players may or may not ante again. If a player opens, the next players in turn have the option of folding, calling, or raising. *Folding* means that a player throws his cards away and has no further financial interest in the pot. *Calling* means that the player bets the same number of chips as the opener. *Raising* means that the player calls and increases the bet. *Overcalling* means that the player makes the second or subsequent call.

All players have a chance to call or to fold. Even if a player has passed and a later player opens the pot, the player who has passed still has an option of calling or raising. To pass and then call when the pot has been opened is called *backing in* the pot.

After the first round of betting is completed, the players who are still in the pot can discard any number of cards and have the dealer give them a new card for each unwanted card. The final hand still consists of five cards.

A second and final round of betting then takes place after the draw, starting with the player who opened on the first round and proceeding as usual to the left around the table.

Once the pot is opened, the winner of the pot is the player who has the best hand and who has made or called the last bet or raise. If a player makes the last bet or raise and is not called, this player wins the whole pot, no matter how miserable a hand he may hold.

It is worth noting the subtle but large difference between the first and last rounds of betting. On the second round a player with a big hand, say Aces-full, might very well pass —hoping that another player will bet and step into his trap —without endangering his right to the pot. However, if a player passes on the first round, the hand may be passed out, and he loses everything except his share of the ante. To pass with a big hand is to *sandbag* in poker parlance. (We will talk more about sandbagging later in this chapter.)

One final ground rule of poker is important: the betting limits. The most liberal game is called *table stakes,* where a player may bet any or all of the chips he has in front of him when the cards are dealt. A *pot-limit* game is very close to a table-stakes game, where a player can bet any amount up to the size of the pot. As the betting proceeds, the pot grows, so that big bets are usually possible. A *limit* game is one in which the maximum size of the bet is determined in advance. Sometimes the limit depends on the round. For example, a $5 to $10 draw game means that the maximum bet is $5 on the first round and $10 on the second round. As long as the betting limit is close to the size of the total ante, there is little difference in opening and calling tactics between a limit and a table-stakes game.

The rules and definitions just given are necessary to playing poker, but they are not sufficient for formulating a winning strategy. Knowing the law does not make a man a wise judge. The following section of this chapter deals with the actual opening and calling strategies of draw poker.

The Importance of the Ante

Assume you are playing draw poker in a game with no ante. What is the proper hand with which to open the betting, and on what hands should you call the opener? The best strategy is surprisingly simple: Never bet, neither open nor call, with anything less than a royal straight flush! You will never lose any money, and you will eventually profit from any player who opens or calls with anything less. An unfortunate side effect of following this ideal strategy, of course, would be acute boredom and perhaps a sudden reduction in your invitations to future poker games.

What our example demonstrates is the oft forgotten truth: **The object of poker is to win the ante.**

The contest for the ante must be given considerable thought. What weapons do you have in your arsenal and what tactics can you devise with which to battle for the ante? When do you use the bomb and when the rapier? The battle in poker resembles real battles and wars in general. Once international disputes pass a certain stage of hostilities, the original limited objectives are often forgotten, and the entire resources of nations are wagered. In poker the objectives and costs must be kept within sight at all times.

Draw poker is almost always played with an ante. In some games of stud, ostensibly without antes, a player in a certain position or with the highest up-card is forced to make a bet. This bet takes the place of an ante. But without some form of ante or forced bet (called a *blind bet*), the game degenerates into a tedious "sit and wait" contest requiring no skill, only patience and *sitzfleisch*. Poker requires an ante to make it a game worth playing.

A game with a large ante is as absurd as a game without any ante. When all the other bets are limited to a small percentage of the mandatory pot, there is no call for finesse. If a player's ante is $10, and the limit on bets is $1, he must stay in the game with almost any sort of hand just to protect his portion of the ante. He has no freedom to maneuver; the game depends entirely on the cards. These games are often played knowing that they require little skill and that the players merely want to gamble blindly.

In a proper poker game the emphasis should be on the ratio of the opening bet to the total ante. The ratio should be close to one. This leads to the most interesting draw games. When there is no ante, the ratio is infinite; when there is a very low limit on the opening bet, the ratio is close to zero. The opening bet should be equal to the total ante. For brevity, hereafter in this book *ante* will always mean the *total ante*.

Probability

How does a player plan reasonable tactics for draw poker? To this end some discussion of probability is in order, and most of the probability must be computed before a player sits down to play; there is far too much going on in a game for a player to stop for complicated computations even if he were so inclined. The computations are included in the tables of this chapter. The reader should understand the deductions that follow from these computed probabilities, not merely the array of numbers.

OPENING HANDS AND THEIR FREQUENCY

In the following discussion we shall analyze the game of draw poker called Jacks or better, in which the opener must have at least a pair of Jacks on the first round. There are no restrictions on the hands of a caller or raiser. This is the most popular version of draw, and the opening strategy developed here applies to almost any other version of draw. The strategic ideas developed are the same for stud, although the corresponding rules must be changed somewhat for that game.

Table 2.1

Distribution of Opening Hands on the First Round

Hands	Number of Hands	Percentage of all Opening Hands
Straight flush or better	40	.007
Four of a kind or better	664	.12
Full house or better	4,408	.8
Flush or better	9,516	1.8
Straight or better	19,716	3.7
Three Kings or better	28,164	5.3
Three 10s or better	40,836	7.6
Three 6s or better	57,732	10.8
Three Deuces or better	74,628	14.0
Aces-up or better	93,630	17.5
Kings-up or better	111,054	20.8
Queens-up or better	126,894	23.7
Jacks-up or better	141,150	26.4
8s-up or better	174,414	32.5
3s-up or better	198,180	37.0
Pair of Aces or better	282,660	52.7
Pair of Kings or better	376,140	68.5
Pair of Queens or better	451,620	84.2
Pair of Jacks or better	536,100	100.0

Five cards are dealt to you at the poker table. What can be said about the hand, even before you look at it? Out of a 52-card deck there are 2,598,960 different five-card combinations. Don't let these large numbers worry you. It is not important to remember the actual numbers but how to use them to formulate a strategy. By "different" I mean that the hands are not identical, card by card. Some hands are so similar that it would appear ridiculous at first glance to call them different: for example, the hand JH, JS, 2H, 3D, 6C, and the hand JH, JS, 2H, 3D, 6S. The two hands are identical except that the 6C in one hand is replaced by the 6S in the other, a seemingly insignificant difference. It is essential that we regard these hands as different, however, if we are going to apply probability, the start of any scientific analysis to poker. Tables 2.1 and 2.2 show how frequently each of the important opening hands in draw poker will occur.

Our major concern in considering draw poker is that there are 536,360 hands containing a pair of Jacks or better (table 2.1). When the cards are dealt, the chance of your getting any one specific hand is equal to that of your getting any other specific hand. Suppose you are dealt an opening hand at Jacks or better. You have one of the 536,360 hands containing a pair of Jacks or better. What is the probability that you will have trip Deuces or better, or a straight or better? According to table 2.1, the probability is .14 for trip Deuces and .037 for a straight or better.

What are the probabilities that you will have at best a pair of Jacks, or at most a pair of Queens? The probability of having a pair of Queens or better is .842, so the probability of having only a pair of Jacks is 1 − .842, or .158. By the same reasoning, the probability of having only a pair of Jacks or Queens is .316.

PROBABILITY OF IMPROVING A HAND IN THE DRAW

Other probabilities are important in playing draw poker: The first set of probabilities determines the five cards dealt

Table 2.2

Hands with Second-Round Potential

Hands	Number of Hands
Four Flushes Four cards in the same suit with an odd card. By drawing one card, you have a 9 in 47 chance of coming up with a flush, about 1 time in 5.	111,540
Four Straight, Open-Ended Four cards in sequence with an odd card. Catching a card on either end of the sequence will make the hand a straight. Chance of making a straight is 8 in 47, or slightly better than 1 time in 6.	257,696
Four-Straight Flush Four cards of the same suit and also in a sequence with a possible gap (i.e., 2S, 3S, 4S, 6S, and KC). By drawing one card there are eight possible spades that will turn the hand into a flush, three possible 5s making the hand a straight, and the 5 of spades turns the hand into a straight flush. Chances of making at least a straight are about 1 in 3 for an open-ended four-straight flush, and about 1 in 4 for an inside four-straight flush. These hands have delightful potential, but unfortunately are almost as rare as full houses.	5,796

in the original hand; the second set of probabilities are the chances of improving your hand in the draw. For example, starting out with a pair of Jacks and drawing three cards, what are the chances of ending up with two pair, trip Jacks, or a full house? Table 2.3 gives the probabilities when drawing down to your hand, that is, drawing three

Table 2.3
Probability of Improving a Hand in the Draw*

First-Round Hand, Drawing to	Second-Round Hand	Probability
A	Quads	.00003
	Full house or better	.00148
	Trips or better	.024
	Two pair or better	.073
	Pair of Aces or better	.25
J, J	Quads	.0028
	Full house or better	.012
	Trips or better	.13
	Two pair or better	.29
	One pair only	.71
J, J, A	Quads	.001
	Full house or better	.06
	Trips or better	.08
	Aces-up or better	.20
	Two pair or better	.26
	One pair only	.73
5, 5, 3, 3	Full house	.085
	Two pair only	.915
2, 2, 2	Quads	.042
	Full house or better	.104
	Trips only	.896
3, 3, 3, 4	Quads	.021
	Full house or better	.085
	Trips only	.915

*Obviously, the player will draw enough cards to complete a five-card hand.

cards to a pair, one card to two pair, and two (or one) card to trips.

Roughly 2 times out of 7 (probability .29) a one-pair hand

improves to two pair or better, 1 time in 8 (probability .13) to trips or better, and 1 time in 80 (probability .012) to a full house or better. In bettor's parlance, the odds are 5 to 2 against improving a pair, 7 to 1 against trips or better, 79 to 1 against a full house or better. However, to avoid the semantic confusion of the prepositions "in" and "to," I prefer to state the odds in terms of probability: .289, .122, or .012.

Now, any poker player who has opened a poker book will have seen these probabilities, and even a bright ten-year old can tell you that the chances of improving two pair to a full house is 4 out of 47. There are forty-seven unseen cards and four of these cards will make a full house from two pair. Therefore, the probability is $\frac{4}{47}$ or .085.

So far we have said nothing profound or given the reader anything new. Let us remedy this by asking and answering the following questions: Given two players—called Players A and B—and their hands before the draw, what is the probability that Player A will have a better hand than Player B after the draw? (See table 2.4.)

Nothing is more frustrating than starting out with a straight and running into another player's full house. Neither player would draw cards; therefore the first player cannot be expected to improve his hand. The first player might win by bluffing, but trying to bluff out a full house is a long shot at best. Similarly, the dread of every player with two pair is to be called on the first round by a player with a higher two pair; here the probability of the first player coming up with the better hand is between .078 and .083, very slim odds.

The most common and slightly more surprising situation is when both players go into the draw with one pair. The player with the higher pair, say Player B, has a commanding lead. The likelihood that Player A will end up with the better

Table 2.4

Probability of Outdrawing One Opponent*

Player A Draws to	Player B Draws to	Probability of Player A Having the Best Hand after the Draw
2, 2	3, 3	.243
	A, A	.230
J, J	A, A	.232
	A, A, K	.243
K, K	A, A	.233
	A, A, K	.181
A, A	A, A	.500
	A, A, K	.213
	3, 3, 2, 2	.265
	2, 2, 2	.114
	2, 2, 2, 3	.117
5, 5, 3, 3	7, 7, 6, 6	.078
	7, 7, 4, 4	.080
	7, 7, 2, 2	.081
	2, 2, 2	.081
	2, 2, 2, 6	.083
2, 2, 2	3, 3, 3	.096
	A, A, A	.096
	3, 3, 3, 4	.098
A	J, J	.210
	2, 2, 3, 3	.067

*Obviously, the player will draw enough cards to complete a five-card hand.

hand is only .233. This is true even in the ridiculous case in which Player A starts out with a pair of Deuces and runs into the second player who only has a pair of 3s.

When the second player has a pair of Aces it does not really matter whether the first player has a pair of Kings or Deuces. The first player's chances only vary from 233 to 230 times in a thousand. Also, Player B, with a pair of Aces, knows that he is going in with the better pair.

You can see from table 2.4 how important it is not to have the worst hand on the first round. Even at Jacks or better, you cannot know with certainty what the opener has, but with certainty calling the opener with a pair of 10s or less is a costly mistake.

Another fact emerges from studying table 2.4. If you are Player B holding trips on the first round against Player A who has either a single pair or two pair, then the question of whether you draw one or two cards makes little difference in your having the better hand after the draw. By drawing two cards you improve your chances only 2 times in a 1,000. Against one opponent, unless there are exceptional circumstances, the information you reveal to the opponent by drawing two cards is usually not justified by the odds.

When on the first round you are Player B, holding a pair of Aces with a King side card against Player A, who is holding only a single pair, you may be justified in holding on to your King and drawing only two cards, even though this action might well reveal your hand. However, this discussion is purely academic, because you will seldom know your opponent's hand.

Let us give the more important set of probabilities when you know only the range of an opponent's hands. For example, the ante is $10, Player A opens the pot for $10. Player B knows that Player A holds a pair of Jacks or better. With what first-round hands does Player B have sufficient odds to justify a $10 call? If Player B has the better hand on the second round, with probability .33 or better, a $10 call is possibly justified. Table 2.5 gives the probabilities of Player B's having the better hand on the second round, assuming that Player A opened whenever he had a pair of Jacks or better and drew to his hand.

Table 2.5

Probability of the First Caller Beating the Opener When the Opener Has a Pair of Jacks or Better

Before the Draw the Caller Has	Probability the Caller Has the Better Hand	
	Before the Draw	After the Draw
10, 10	–	.191
J, J	.015	.201
Q, Q	.166	.286
K, K	.347	.432
A, A	.528	.509
3, 3, 2, 2	.631	.513

Remember, Player B must have at least a .33 probability of having a stronger hand than Player A in order to call. A pair of Kings gives sufficient odds (.432) for Player B to enter the pot, and certainly a pair of Aces (.509), or two little pair (.513) qualify as calling hands against the opener. A pair of Queens or less does not justify calling against a player who has opened with Jacks or better. The probability of beating him with a pair of Queens is .286, with a pair of Jacks, .201, and with lower than Jacks—barring a bluff—.191 or less. Even if your opponent is a miserable player, the deck cannot know he is a dunce. Brute chance will give him a commanding lead in the draw.

Table 2.5 implies one of the first calling rules: **Never call the opener with less than a pair of Kings.** When to call with a pair of Kings depends on several factors, such as the number of players who have not yet acted on their hands, the position of the opener, and so forth. These topics will be discussed later in this chapter.

Opening Rules

WHEN TO OPEN WITH A PAIR OF JACKS

The only blind gamble at poker is when you ante. You have seen no cards and yet, to be in the game at all, you must make the initial ante. At this stage nothing is guaranteed. From this one blind moment on, however, wagers can be placed with precisely calculated risks and benefits.

For reference, the player immediately to the left of the dealer, under the gun, has Position 1, the next player to the left has Position 2, and so forth. In a five-handed game, the dealer will have Position 5.

Suppose you are the first player to the left of the dealer, Position 1, in a five-handed Jacks-or-better game. The total ante is $10. You look at your hand and see that you have a pair of Jacks, so you open the pot for $10. What are the various results? (1) All the other players fold after you have opened, and you win the $10 ante. (2) One or more of the remaining players call your bet. The first caller must have at least a pair of Kings. If called by one or more players, your meager pair of Jacks is a long shot for the pot, but with improvement in the draw, they could be a possible winner.

The probability of any player having a calling hand can be computed. More to the point, the amount of money won or lost in each situation can be calculated. By such devices, you can determine whether you would make or lose money by opening with a pair of Jacks. We simplify this computation by asking what the probability is that none of the remaining four players has a pair of Kings or better. Remember an opponent knows only that you have *at least* a pair of Jacks, and so at the very least he needs a pair of Kings before he can make a profitable call. The probability of any player having a pair of Kings or better is .141; thus, the probability that a given player does *not* have a pair of Kings or better is .859. The probability that none of the four remaining players has a pair of Kings or better is .544. You will win the ante outright, i.e., without being called, over half the time, in fact around 5 times out of 9.

It is obvious from this analysis that it is profitable to open the pot with a pair of Jacks in any position in a five-handed game. Remember, no other player knows that you have only a pair of Jacks. Your opponents only know that you have at least a pair of Jacks. With any hand higher than a pair of Jacks, of course, it is even more profitable to open.

In a method similar to the one used for a five-handed game, the minimal opening hand can be computed when playing in a six-, seven-, or eight-handed game. The minimal opening hand for each game is given in table 2.6. If you open with any weaker hand, you are courting a loss. However, as table 2.6 shows, the game is too subtle for you to automatically open just because you have the minimally required pair

Table 2.6
Opening Rules: Minimal Hands for Jacks or Better

Position of Opener								
Game	1	2	3	4	5	6	7	8
Five-Handed	JJ	JJ	JJ	JJ	JJ	–	–	–
Six-Handed	Pass*	QQ or JJA	JJ	JJ	JJ	JJ	–	–
Seven-Handed	Pass	Pass	KK or QQA	QQ or JJA	JJ	JJ	JJ	–
Eight-Handed	Pass	Pass	Pass	KK or QQA	QQ or JJA	JJ	JJ	JJ

*Pass means that a player in this position passes *all* hands (sandbags).

of Jacks. As we shall see, there are situations in which it is wisest to pass even though you could open the betting.

SANDBAGGING IN THE OPENING

Sandbagging means that a player passes with a high hand rather than opening. Watching a poker player with a big hand who lies in wait for his fellow players, refusing to open and passing on full houses with a nonchalant air, is like watching an acrobat on film. Only the spectacular swoops and jumps that succeed are seen; the times when the acrobat falters are edited out. Similarly, you never know on a passed-out hand when the full house takes a pratfall.

Sandbagging is an important tactic in opening, but it is effective only if done in the right circumstances and with the greatest care. Many players will open the betting with any hand from a pair of Jacks through two medium-sized pair but will sandbag with any higher hand. When these players do open, they become overly vulnerable to a first-round raise, and they have no ammunition left when the fighting becomes

35

hot in the first round. The advantages of sandbagging for the different types of hands are as follows:

1. With a pair of Kings or Aces, when the pot is later opened but not raised, you have a profitable call. On the second round you are in a much better betting position than if you had opened. Remember, because the opener starts off the second-round betting, he has a strategic disadvantage. You hope to catch the opener with a pair of Jacks or Queens. The minimal calling hand is a pair of Kings. Therefore if you catch a pair of Queens opening, you have a clear advantage. Theoretically and usually in practice, if you open, the pair-of-Queens player will not call. If you are unfortunate enough to run into a two pair or trips, you still have a chance to have the best hand after the draw. If the hand is opened and raised before it is your turn to act, you can gracefully withdraw, folding with relief that you hadn't opened.

2. With a two-pair hand you can again profitably call when the pot is opened and not raised. You can also profitably call with a limited number of four flushes because the opener cannot tell the nature of your hand when you draw one card.

3. With trips or better you can profitably raise the opener. The profit on these high hands depends upon whether the game is strict-limit poker or not.

It has been shown that it is possible to open the betting with a pair of Jacks. However, is it more profitable to sandbag with a high hand? There is a good chance the hand will be passed out. (The argument against sandbagging, in fact, is that this possibility exists; when there are five remaining potential openers, the chances are about 7 out of 10 that the pot will be opened.) The difficulty is that if you pass as first man in a five-handed game, there is about a 40 percent chance that none of the remaining four players will even be able to open. Furthermore, a timid opponent may not open even with a pair of Jacks. As a result, about 4 times out of 10 the pot will not be opened. In the remaining 6 times, when the pot is opened, you can raise. However, it is still more profitable to open than to sandbag when there are only four remaining openers.

In a six-handed game, with six players in the pot, the minimal opening hand for the first player is a pair of Queens. However, in this case it is advantageous for the player under the gun (Position 1) to sandbag. (Position 1 is the man to the left of the dealer, Position 2 is two players to the left of the dealer, and so on.) If the player in Position 1 passes, the player in Position 2 must take into account that Position 1 might be sandbagging. For the second man to open he must have a minimal hand that will stand up against five potential callers—a pair of Queens or better. If the player in Position 2 has the minimal opening hand, he should not sandbag. Although the Position 2 man has five potential callers if he opens, when he passes there are only four potential openers. The Position 2 player makes more money by opening than by passing, because the likelihood of the hand being passed out is too great. Any player from Position 3 on should open if he has a pair of Jacks or better.

When the player in Position 2 passes, the game reverts to a five-man game, and a pair of Jacks qualifies as an opener. Two rather interesting phenomena emerge when comparing the opening strategies of a five-handed game and a six-handed game: First, in a five-handed game the player under the gun is at the greatest disadvantage. If he has a pair of Jacks or better he should open, and then four other players can try to wrest the pot away from him. In a six-handed game, the man in Position 1 has an advantage over the man in Position 2. Second, in a five-handed game the probability that no one has a pair of Jacks or better is about .31; there is about a 7 out of 10 chance that the pot will be opened. In a six-handed game the probability that no one will have a pair of Jacks or better is .24; the player in Position 1 should automatically pass, and the second man should open only if he has a pair of Queens or better. Thus, in a six-handed game there are only five potential openers and the first potential opener needs a pair of Queens or better. If the players are playing in their best interest, the chances of a six-handed game being opened are less than in a five-handed game. However, in a six-handed game the chances of the opener being called increase considerably, making a six-handed game far more interesting than a five-handed game.

The rules for a seven- and eight-handed game are very similar to those of a six-handed game except that the players in the first two or three positions should automatically pass. The opening hands in a seven- or eight-handed game are presented in table 2.6.

Before leaving the opener's strategy, some mention of an opener's side cards is in order. For example, it is much better to open with J, J, A, K, 2 than with Q, Q, 2, 3, 4 because the chances of running into a pair of Aces or Kings is reduced 50 percent. The first hand has a much better chance of walking off with the ante by opening than does the second hand. Also, the possession of the side cards will be valuable information for second-round betting.

Calling Rules

Rules for the first caller. When the pot has been opened at Jacks or better, the immediate concern is the opener, but some thought should be given to the other players as well. For example, in a five-handed game, the opener is in Position 1 (sitting immediately to the left of the dealer). If you are the dealer in Position 5, you could call with a weaker hand than if you were in Position 2. When you are the dealer, you will have heard from all of the other players. In Position 2 there remain three players, any one of whom could possibly have a big hand. Calling the opener with a pair of Kings and then being raised by a third player is financially painful. Being overcalled by a pair of Aces is also unpleasant.

Table 2.7

Calling Rules: Minimal Hands for the First and Second Callers at Jacks or Better in a Five-Handed Game

	First Caller*			
Position of Opener	Position of First Caller and Minimal Calling Hands			
	2	3	4	5
1	KKA	KK	KK	KKJ
2	–	KKA	KK	KK
3	–	–	KK	KK
4	–	–	–	KK
	Second Caller*			

The second caller *must* have either a pair of Aces or two pair.
(In a very tight game, do *not* call with two pair less than 8s-up if the side card is a face card.)

*The first and second caller also call with all four-straight flushes and all A-K, A-Q, and A-J high four flushes.

A pair of Kings is the usual minimal calling hand, but there is another useful aid for determining your call. When you have a pair of Kings, you also have three side cards. The side cards can give you important information about the opener. For example, if you have the hand K, K, 2, 7, 8, you know very little about the opener's hand other than it is unlikely that he has a pair of Kings. If you have the hand K, K, A, 2, 7, your possession of the Ace lowers by 50 percent the probability that the opener has Aces. Thus, the hand K, K, A, x, x is much stronger than the hand K, K, x, x, x, although in drawing you should throw away the Ace and draw three cards. Another asset of the hand K, K, A, x, x is that it lowers the odds of your being overcalled by a pair of Aces.

Table 2.8

Calling Rules: Minimal Hands for the First and Second Callers at Jacks or Better in a Six-Handed Game

	First Caller*				
Position of Opener	Position of First Caller and Minimal Calling Hands				
	2	3	4	5	6
1	AA	AA	KKA	KK	KK
2	–	AA	KKA	KK	KK
3	–	–	KKA	KK	KK
4	–	–	–	KK	KK
5	–	–	–	–	KK
	Second Caller*				

In Position 3 or 4 call with 9s-up or better.
In Position 5 or 6 call with a pair of Aces, all two pair.

*The first and second caller also call with all four-straight flushes and all A-K, A-Q, and A-J high four flushes.

40

The hands K, K, Q, x, x and K, K, J, x, x are definitely weaker than the hand K, K, 2, 7, 8 for now your possession of a Q (or J) lowers the probability by 50 percent that the opener has a pair of Queens (or a pair of Jacks). As a caller, the worst possible pair of Kings you could have is K, K, Q, J, x, making the odds almost 50 percent that if the opener has a pair at all, it's a pair of Aces.

With a pair of Kings and the correct side cards you can give yourself enough of an edge to compensate for the risk of overcalls or raises from those players left to speak. If the opening bet is the size of the ante, the hand K, K, A, x, x always qualifies as a calling hand. Never call with the hand K, K, Q, J, x. Tables 2.7, 2.8, and 2.9 give the calling rules for a five-, six-, or seven-handed game.

Table 2.9

Calling Rules: Minimal Hands for the First and Second Callers at Jacks or Better in a Seven-Handed Game

	First Caller*					
Position of Opener	Position of First Caller and Minimal Calling Hands					
	2	3	4	5	6	7
1	AA	AA	AA	AA	AA	AA
2	–	AA	AA	KKA	KKA	KK
3	–	–	KKA	KKA	KK	KK
4	–	–	–	KKA	KK	KK
5	–	–	–	–	KK	KK
6	–	–	–	–	–	KK

Second Caller*

In Positions 3 or 4 call with 8s-up or better. In Position 5, 6, or 7 call with a pair of Aces and any two pair.

*The first and second caller also call with all four-straight flushes and all A-K, A-Q, and A-J high four flushes.

41

It is important to emphasize that no cards be flashed or shown by any of the players. If the pot is opened, a potential caller will have a tremendous advantage if he is able to see his neighbor's hand, say a neighbor who is passing out of the hand and has no further interest in the pot. The knowledge derived from seeing an extra five cards is a veritable bonanza for a player with a borderline calling hand.

A pair of Aces and two pair certainly qualify as calling hands. As profitable as two pair are, a little thought should be given to them with respect to the second round of betting. The chances of improving to a full house are slight, only about 1 in 12 (See table 2.3). In the first round if you are going to call with two pair and raise with trips (the correct procedure), then when you call and draw only one card, your hand is pretty well marked for two pair. Even if the opener starts with only a pair and draws three cards, he can then bet with any high two pair or better with comparative safety.

We have not yet discussed bluffing. Accompanying the high-hand bets, of course, will be the corresponding number of bluffs. Thus, two pair becomes a defensive hand, vulnerable to aggressive betting by the opener. The caller should try to find some way of disguising his calling hands and the obvious way to do this is by calling with a certain number of four flushes. The situation in which the opener squares off against a four flush and knows what he is up against is discussed in chapter 3. The opener's tactic is to pass automatically to the potential flush and to call a certain percent of the time. With these tactics the four flush does not usually win enough money to make a first-round call worthwhile.

The tactics of the opener against two pair are almost the opposite of the correct tactics against a four flush. Hence, if the caller uses both two pair and four flushes to call, he will strengthen his two-pair hands. Calling with four flushes is weak when the opener knows that you are calling with a four flush. But if you have not yet passed, call and draw only one card; the opener will not know whether you are calling with a four flush or two pair. You are effectively neutralizing any information in the draw.

Tables 2.7, 2.8, and 2.9 give the correct strategy for the caller, giving both a mixture of two pair and four flushes. If the ante is $10, the pot is opened for $10, and you call for $10, the pot now contains $30 and becomes attractive to four flushes. Therefore, the four flushes that the first caller uses are the highest possible four flushes. If you are overcalled by a four flush, you will have a good chance of coming out with the highest flush.

In a six-, seven-, or eight-handed game where the pot has been opened by one of the players not in Positions 1 or 2, the calling rules for either the first or second callers are the same as in a five-handed game. Neither the reasons for the calls nor the odds shift significantly from a five-handed to a six-handed game. The only difference is if the opener is in Positions 1 or 2, then all of the calls must be tightened.

Overcalling rules for the second and subsequent callers on the first round. When the pot has been opened and called, the pot presents interesting odds to any subsequent player.

Suppose you are playing in a five-handed game and the pot has been opened and called by Players A and B. You are not overly concerned with running into big hands from the two players who have not yet acted; in all likelihood either one or both of them will fold. What are your chances of coming up with the best hand on the second round, knowing that Player A has an opening hand and Player B has a first calling hand?

The ante is $10, Player A opens for $10, Player B calls for $10, so if you call for $10 the pot will contain $40. You are off and running in a good sized pot, but is your horse fast enough for this race? Will you have at least a 1 in 4 chance of coming up with the best hand in the second round? In poker, there is no prize for coming in second.

Table 2.10

Probability of the Second Caller Having the Best Hand When the Opener Has a Pair of Jacks or Better and the First Caller Has a Pair of Kings or Better

Before the Draw the Second Caller Has	Probability the Second Caller Has the Best Hand After the Draw
10, 10	.14
J, J	.16
Q, Q	.17
K, K	.24
A, A	.30
3, 3, 2, 2	.28

Table 2.10 shows that a pair of Aces gives about a 3 in 10 chance of winning, certainly a qualifying hand. A pair of Kings is less than a 1 in 4 chance—just not good enough, so this old plug should be scratched from the race. **A pair of Kings does not qualify as a calling hand for the second caller.**

Two small pair give barely enough odds: 8s-up or less qualify only if the side card is not a face card. If the side card is a face card or an Ace, it lowers the probability that both Player A and Player B have only one pair, so it correspondingly raises the probability that at least one of these players has a higher two pair. Starting with two small pair and hitting a full house on the draw is a long shot, 4 in 47, so that most likely you will be in round two with two small pair, a most uncomfortable situation against two players.

Of course, any four-straight flush admirably qualifies for the second or subsequent callers. Some players give first-round raises with a four-straight flush, a mistake. The hand is too strong for a bluff hand; it is a genuine calling hand. But it is not strong enough for a raise hand.

As we have seen, a limited number of four-flush hands come into play for the first caller and equally qualify for the second caller. Actually, the four flush is a very marginal hand for the second caller. As we shall see later, these hands have a much better use as bluff raise hands.

For the third and subsequent caller, four-flush hands are profitable first-round calling hands. A pair of Aces and two small pair less than 10s-up do not qualify as calling hands. For later callers, the rules loosen up in some ways and tighten in others.

Hereafter in this book, the opener will be called Player A, the first caller Player B, the second caller Player C, and so forth.

The calling rules for players subsequent to Player C are:

All two pair from Aces-up to 10s-up.

All four flushes.

45

Observations on Opening and Calling

The purpose behind opening is to systematically steal the ante. When you open the pot with a pair of Jacks, Queens, or Kings (and these are about one-half of your opening hands), you are not particularly comfortable about being called. If you are going to open the pot you should open it not just with the "ante stealers" but with the better hands. Then if you are called or raised you will have protection and your big hands will profitably come into the action.

One of the assumptions used in computing whether or not it is profitable to open with a pair of Jacks is that no one would come into the pot with less than a pair of Kings. Suppose, however, that you open and are called by a player with a pair of Queens. You will certainly be hurt if you have only a pair of Jacks and the Jacks will show a loss. But this loss will be amply compensated when you have a pair of Kings or better. Any player who calls with a pair of Queens will show an overall loss, and the loss will go to the opener. Or suppose that you open and are called by a player with a short pair (10s or less). The caller has taken long odds to outdraw you, but now you have an unexpected bonus, making opening a pleasant pastime.

Another assumption is that a player will open when it is more profitable for him to do so than to sandbag. For example, in a six-man game you are in Position 5 and the players in Positions 1, 2, 3, and 4 have passed. In deciding whether or not to open, you assume that the player in Position 1 may be sandbagging but that the players in Positions 2, 3, and 4 do not have opening hands. However, suppose they fool you and are sandbagging whenever they can. Certainly opening now on a pair of Jacks becomes more risky and you will show a slight loss. But, what you lose in opening with a pair of Jacks is proportionately returned to you on your poor hands when the hand is passed out and you get your ante back. What is important is to maximize the profit over all of your hands.

In a Jacks-or-better game the rules automatically give minimal protection to a weak player in the opening, but the rules offer no shelter to the subsequent callers. The amount of money a player will throw away being the first, or even subsequent, caller with a pair of Queens or Jacks or less becomes substantial over the course of time. The loss in any one hand is not great. In fact, he could come out a winner a few times, but the long-term loss is there and the opportunity presents itself so frequently that it is probably the main flaw in a weak player's game. The temptation to get in a $40 pot for only $10 is often just too much to resist for the sport holding a pair of 10s.

The rules given in this chapter may seem severe, especially in a friendly game, but my advice is: Stick to them. It may be your money that makes the game so friendly.

In an eight-handed game, both the calling and opening rules are, by necessity, quite stringent. This fact is recognized in most private games where the game is usually limited to seven players. At a public poker casino the profit is made from charging chair rent to the players: A club prefers to crowd eight players around the table. As draw poker cannot accommodate more than eight players, alas, the casinos have started promoting the game of "hold 'em," using a slightly larger table and a game that can accommodate twelve players.

CHAPTER 3

Bluffing: The Optimal Strategy in Draw Poker

Bluff: To deceive (an opponent in cards) by a bold bet on an inferior hand with the result that the opponent drops a winning hand; . . . to deter, dissuade, or frighten by pretence or a mere show of strength; . . . to cause to believe what is not true.

Webster's Third International Dictionary

The Optimal Strategy

For every situation in poker there is an optimal strategy. All the basic reasoning and poker table tactics for the particular case of the opener versus the four flush are given in the following discussion. Later in the book, where the more general rules are given, the underlying reasons will get only a passing mention. The full discussion is given here because a player who understands the reasoning behind the optimal strategy will be a better poker player.

A strategy is a plan, a predetermined set of rules for the employment of forces to achieve a given aim. In draw poker a strategy is a set of rules by which a player decides how to employ the various sorts of hands he is likely to hold—when to bet, how much to bet, how many cards to draw, and so forth. What is the aim of such a strategy in poker? The simplest answer would be: To make money. But a little further thought leads to the more complex answer: To guarantee the most money possible. Unfortunately, no strategy can guarantee the most money possible because in order to make the most money possible you would have to win every hand. Thus we turn to a practical answer: To yield the maximum guaranteeable profit over the long run. This, in effect, is the optimal strategy in poker.

One further consideration must be kept in mind. Does the efficacy of any strategy depend on the opponent's strategy? For example, to achieve maximum effectiveness, when you know that your opponent almost never bluffs, wouldn't you call him much less often than the man you know is a habitual bluffer? The answer is yes, if you know these things you would adjust your strategy accordingly. But, you seldom know such things for sure.

Sometimes there are one or two unknown players in the game; then you will want the best strategy to deal with their unpredictable play. At other times, against really good players, your ability to "read" their hands and their habits is reduced drastically. Sometimes you may be able to learn something about their betting habits and playing styles, but most of the time you will be playing with no inkling of your opponent's thinking. As a result you will probably be making your decisions based on the most capricious kinds of intuition and guesswork, calling it, of course, "card sense." You may win a bundle playing this way, but you may also take a bath. There is no guarantee at all in this kind of capricious playing. Not only is there no guarantee, the player who follows such whimsy takes on some real liabilities. Some of them may be expensive, some may merely detract from the pleasures of the game. For one thing, there is no order to such a capricious game. Whether he wins or loses remains forever beyond the player's control. This is especially serious when he is playing a losing strategy. Since he cannot know what he is doing, he cannot know what he is doing wrong. This can cost a good bit of money—money that cannot even be considered invested in a learning experience. The capricious player does not learn.

What is needed, then, is a set of playing rules clearly worked out before the game. To devise such a strategy you can work only with information you can rely on—not luck, not the psychological quirks of the opposition. You can rely only on probabilities and on your own skill in exploiting them.

The optimal strategy in poker is the one that brings the maximum guaranteeable profit over the long run when you are confronted with opponents whose responding strategies you cannot predict. The strategy given in this book assumes opponents who are good players. If they are not good players, you can read what they are likely to do and there is no need for any strategy. In a game played by masters, however, a strategy is the only defense you have against the whims of chance and the expertise of your opponents.

The profit from this strategy is guaranteeable in the sense that no matter what your opponents do, they will not be able to reduce the profitability of your strategy in a given situation. It will be the maximum profit only insofar as it is guaranteeable: You might be able to achieve a greater profit by taking certain chances or by acting on your knowledge of how your opponent plays, but your methods are not guaranteed.

The strategy provides both offense and defense. Many common poker situations are conflicts in which one player in a stronger betting position is the aggressor. The other player is then forced to make a defensive but judicious call or fold. These situations can be analyzed as a clash between two different strategies. We will describe the offensive strategy that will bring the maximum guaranteeable profit to the stronger hand and the defensive strategy that will minimize loss for the weaker hand. The defensive strategy will guarantee that the offensive player cannot possibly gain any more than a certain amount. If the offensive player plays his hand badly, (not all poker players will have read this book), the defender may end up gaining the upper hand.

The Opener versus the Four Flush

These general observations will be made clearer by the following example:

The game is five-handed, pot-limit, Jacks or better. On the first round the first four players pass and the pot is opened by Player A in Position 5, in this case the dealer. Player B, sitting in Position 4 immediately to the right of the dealer, is the only caller. The pot now contains $12. Player B draws one card.

Since B originally passed in Position 4, called only after A had opened, and then drew one card, it is almost certain that

B has a four flush or a four straight. The opener does not care which hand B actually has because the opener's play is identical in both situations. For the purposes of the example, let us assume that B has a four flush before the draw.

The chances of B's hitting his flush in the draw are about 1 in 5. There are nine cards in the remaining forty-seven that would give him the flush. Put aside for a moment the question of whether or not B should have come into the hand at all under the given circumstances.

Player B's hand has the potential for both offensive and defensive strategies. In this case the reader understands that B is on the offense and A is on the defense. Considering the $12 in the pot to be nobody's money at this stage (and again putting aside the question of how much B invested to get this far), if B follows his optimal strategy, he can guarantee himself a profit over the long run.

THE OPTIMAL STRATEGY FOR THE FOUR FLUSH

Let's assume that A, the opener, does the apparently reasonable thing and passes to B's one-card draw. Player B will do one of three things: (1) If he has made his flush, he will bet the size of the pot, $12 in this case. If he has not made his flush, he will either (2) pass or (3) bluff, again betting $12. As we have just seen, he will make the flush once every five times ($\frac{9}{47}$) so that 80 percent of the time B will find himself with a busted four flush. More often than not he will be asking himself the question: What shall I do now?

What happens if B decides he is never going to bluff? He will bet only when he has made his flush; when he is busted he will always pass. For the sake of our calculations we are forced to make a few assumptions, hoping they will not seem unreasonable to the reader. We will assume, for one thing, that if B makes his flush he is a winner. It is conceivable, of course, that A has outdrawn B by hitting, say, a full house, but the chances of this are small. Therefore we will assume that if B busts he is a loser. It is conceivable that he could have hit a pair of Aces or Kings and that A has only a pair of Queens, but that stroke of luck is balanced by the possibility that A has filled.

If B bets after the draw only when he has flushed, how much will his average four-flush hand be worth? That depends on how often Player A calls him. If A is a timid player who never calls B in this situation, the following will happen: Every ten times B draws to his four flush, eight times he will bust and pass and twice he will make the flush and bet the size of the pot, $12 in our example. Because A is not calling him, B will be allowed to take the $12 pot twice in ten hands. His profit (still putting aside consideration of how much he had to pay to call in the first place) over ten hands is $24— an average of $2.40 per hand.

Assume now that instead of A's never calling a post-draw bet by B, Player A always calls. What happens to B if he continues his strategy of never bluffing? Again, B will bust and pass eight out of ten times. Twice he will bet $12 and twice A will call with $12 and both times B will win. Only this time he will be winning $24 per hand—the $12 pot plus A's call of $12. In ten hands B will win $48—an average of $4.80 per hand. If B has decided that he is never going to bluff he should hope that A has decided to call all the time. Unfortunately B cannot count on A's calling all the time. Chances are that after getting clobbered six or eight times in a row when B bets and A calls, A will learn to apply his always-call policy a little more loosely. To the extent that B cannot count on this, his profit is not guaranteeable.

There is a system of bluffing that guarantees B a profit of $3.60 per hand. The system of never bluffing could bring $4.80 but it could also bring only $2.40. Since the other player is likely to notice that B never bluffs he will probably adjust his own playing strategy in such a way that B's winnings will eventually tend to be closer to the minimal $2.40 than to the maximum $4.80.

How will B do if he never bluffs and A calls him half the time? Player B will bet only when he has flushed and, as we have seen, he will flush twice in every ten four-flush hands. Once B will bet $12, A will call, and B will win $24—the $12 pot plus A's $12 call. Once B will bet $12, A will fold, and B will win $12—the pot that A allows B to take uncontested. This means that B would be profiting $36 over ten hands, averaging $3.60 per hand if he never bluffs and if A calls half the time. But since he can't count on A's calling half the time (remember, if A never calls, B would average only $2.40 per hand) this is anything but a guaranteed $3.60.

A second possible system for B to adopt would be to bluff all of the time. Of each ten four flushes he draws, he makes his flush twice. Two of his ten bets would be strength bets; that is, he will have made his flush. According to this strategy, he still bets the other eight times when he draws one card and busts. How does he fare? Alas, this is another system with no guarantee because it depends on how often A calls. If A never calls, B bets $12 ten times in ten four-flush hands and is allowed each time to take the $12 pot. That makes $120 or an average of $12 per hand. A fine average! But what happens when A catches on and starts calling all the time? Player B catches A twice when B actually has the flush and wins $24 each time. This puts B ahead $48. But B will bet $12 the other eight times and lose it every time A calls. As a result, B loses $96. B's net for the ten hands is minus $48—he loses an average of $4.80 per hand. This is a likely outcome because if B bluffs all the time, the other players will soon catch on and call him.

What will happen to B if he bluffs all the time and A calls him half the time? On the two flushes he completes, B will win a total of $36—$24 when A calls and loses, $12 when A folds. Of the other eight times when B bluff bets $12, A will call half the time and B will lose his $12 bet, and A will fold half the time and B will win the $12 pot. On the bluffs, then, B will make nothing at all—zero profit, and zero loss. This means that he will again make $36 over the ten hands —an average of $3.60 per hand.

By this same sort of analysis we find that if B bluffs, say, twice for every strength bet (of the ten four-flush hands, he bets twice, bluffs four times, and passes four times) he will profit $7.20 per hand if A never calls, $3.60 if A calls half the time, and nothing if A always calls.

Some interesting patterns emerge from these figures. Probability tables are probably more interesting to the professional mathematician than to the professional poker player, but table 3.1 contains information that should intrigue any serious poker player. It summarizes what happens to B's profits as he varies the frequency of his bluffing and A varies the frequency of his calling. For example, table 3.1 shows that if A has a policy of never calling, Player B's profits rise the more he bluffs. Also, if A has a policy of always calling, Player B's profits decrease the more he bluffs.

This illustration of B squaring off against A can now lead

us to a guaranteed maximum profit strategy for Player B. Table 3.1 reveals that when B always bluffs, his winnings depend on how often A calls. The profits are high when A never calls and negative when A always calls. Player B's profits when he never bluffs are also shown. Notice that the profit is low when A never calls and high when A always calls. Player B's profits are still dependent on A's calling policy.

Table 3.1

Player B's Profit: When Players A and B Vary Their Strategies

Player B Bluffs	Player A Calls		
	Never	50 Percent	Always
Always	$12.00	$3.60	− $4.80
2:1*	7.20	3.60	0
1:1	4.80	3.60	2.40
1:2	3.60	3.60	3.60
Never	2.40	3.60	4.80

*2:1 means that Player B makes two bluffs for every strength bet.

We see that B's profits fluctuate wildly as each player varies his strategy. Does Player B have a strategy that will both be unaffected by Player A's unpredictable strategy and earn the most money possible against a tough opponent? Such a strategy brings Player B the *largest guaranteeable profit*—that is exactly what constitutes an optimal strategy.

Remember in what sense B's profit is optimal, but not necessarily maximal. Player B could make $12 per hand if he always bluffed and A never called. This possible profit is far larger than the optimal profit, but here the word "optimal" includes the idea of "guaranteeable." In this simple example the optimal strategy yields a profit considerably less than the maximal $12 per hand. However, you can think of the difference in winnings as insurance. The optimal strategy is a safe way to always make $3.60, not a risky way sometimes to make $12.

What happens to B when he adopts a bluff-to-strength ratio of 1:2, that is, he bluffs once for every two times he makes a strength bet? Out of ten four-flush hands he will flush twice and bet them both. Eight times he will bust, and of those eight times he will pass seven times and bluff bet one time. Notice how this works. Suppose A never calls. This means that B will flush twice and bet $12, he will bust once and bet $12, and the other seven times he will pass. Each time B bets $12, A folds to him and B wins the $12 pot—making $36 in all, or $3.60 per hand. Suppose A always calls. This means that B will flush twice, bet $12 and win—profiting $24 each time (the pot plus A's calling bet)—and B will bust once and bluff bet $12, which he will lose to A's call. The $48 won minus the $12 lost gives B $36 again—he has maintained his profit at $3.60 per hand. If A calls just half the time, on half the bluffs A will fold and B will win $12; but on the other half A will call and B will lose $12. B's profit still averages $3.60 per hand.

Conclusion: **The optimal strategy in B's four-flush situation is offensive strategy, in which B adopts a bluff ratio of 1:2, that is, one bluff bet for every two strength bets. If B does this, A can do nothing to prevent him from winning an average profit of $3.60 per hand.**

Thus, for poker players Game Theory bears fruit. Game Theory tells us that for every recognizable poker situation we can name, there is an optimal strategy. The strategy may be too complex for us to discern, but in theory there is one.

OPTIMAL STRATEGY FOR THE OPENER

We have not quite finished analyzing the opener versus the four-flush situation. You will recall that there are two conflicting strategies in these situations. One is optimal offensive strategy and the other is optimal defensive strategy. We have already given B's best strategy, which is to take the offensive. But what about A? Another look at table 3.1 reveals his optimal strategy.

Player A's problem is the opposite of B's. Player A can adopt a policy of always calling B, never calling, or calling with some frequency in between. According to table 3.1, we see that if Player A always calls there's a chance he can belt B for an extra $4.80 per hand. But, of course, this is entirely dependent on B's strategy. If B is never bluffing instead of always bluffing, A will end up getting belted himself. Player A is looking for a strategy that is optimal in precisely the same sense as B's strategy: a strategy that will provide him with the best guaranteeable outcome. It turns out that his optimal strategy in this situation is to call half the time. Look at table 3.1 again and notice the center column of figures. These figures tell what happens to B's profit when A calls half the time. Notice that it stays at $3.60 per hand no matter what B does to try to raise it. By calling half the time, A puts a limit on how much B can win. By taking some chances, A might be able to bruise B, but it is more likely that A will get hurt himself. If you are completely uncertain of what the other player is going to do, the optimal strategy is the one that brings the largest guaranteeable profit when you have the upper hand and holds your opponent to the smallest guaranteeable gain when he has the edge.

Notice that B's optimal strategy guarantees him a gain of

$3.60 per hand, while A's optimal strategy guarantees that he, A, will hold B to a gain of $3.60 per hand. The $3.60 figure serves to confirm that both A and B have indeed come up with their optimal strategies. The interpretation is this: If B has an offensive strategy that guarantees him no less than $3.60 per hand, it is a comfort to A to see that his defensive strategy holds B to no more than $3.60. In other words, A can stop B from gaining any more than the guaranteeable profit.

Player A—criteria for calling. The optimal strategy for B is to bet the pot with the bluff-to-strength ratio of 1:2 and for Player A to call B half the time. We will now incorporate these ideas into concrete poker rules.

For a rule to be useful at the poker table, it must be subtle enough to be undetected by your opponents. There must be no indication, for example, that you are bluffing or that you might call a bet. If your optimal strategy is so obvious that everyone knows when you will bluff, the whole theory becomes a farce. Also a rule must be fairly easy to remember. If the rule for bluffing is so complicated that no player can remember when to apply it, the rule is useless as a guide for actual play. Player A must have a practical method of calling Player B's bet half the time. One possibility would be to call every other bet by B, but there is a good chance that B might very well catch on to such a pattern. One way for A to make his behavior a little less predictable is for him to flip a coin for each decision: Heads, A calls; tails, A folds. The probability of a coin showing heads is one in two; the probability of a coin showing tails is one in two. Overall, A will call B's bet half the time, and there is no way of telling in advance which way the coin will fall. I once saw a young gambler in Emeryville, California, use this coin-flipping system. In certain situations he pulled out a coin or, sometimes, a small spinning device to determine whether or not to call a bet. He probably had a sound enough system, but his ego took a terrible beating. After being stung by the other players' jokes at his expense, he admitted to me that he actually preferred chess to poker.

There is a more effective method, especially for the development of the optimal strategy in more complicated situations: **Player A should call with the top one-half of his hands.**

Let us trace the play and give the one-half calling rule in poker terms. In the draw Player A draws down to his hand, that is, A draws three cards to a pair, one card to two pair, and two cards to trips. In this particular situation there is no point for A to try to disguise his hand because if Player B makes his flush he certainly has a powerful hand, a hand well worth a bet. Once A has drawn cards, he has given away information about his hand; he must not let this information give his opponents any clue as to whether he is going to call or fold. Namely, if A draws one card he must call with exactly the same frequency as when he draws three cards. To nullify any information about his plans for calling, Player A must have separate calling rules depending on the number of cards that he draws. The method for deriving the calling rules is quite elementary. If we look at table 3.2, we can find the top 50 percent of A's hands after the draw. The hands are grouped in columns as to whether A draws three, one, or two cards. Looking down the columns to find the top 50 percent of the hands, we arrive at the following calling rules for Player A:

If A draws three cards, A calls with a pair of Aces or better.

If A draws one card, A calls with two pair, Queens-up or better.

If A draws two cards, A calls with three 9s or better.

The above rules are certainly easy enough to remember; however they are slightly inaccurate. Real life is usually sloppier than pure theory. A pair of Aces or better includes only 47 percent of the top hands, not 50 percent, so to be absolutely precise, Player A should call with K, K, A, Q, x or better. Similarly, with two pair the exact rule would be two pair of Jacks and 10s or better. These refinements are hair-splitting and, while they may be of theoretical interest

Table 3.2

Distribution of the Opener's Hands After the Draw

Hands	Opener Draws* Three Cards	Opener Draws One Card	Opener Draws Two Cards
Full house or better	.013	.085	.147
Three Kings or better	.066		.257
Three Jacks or better	.127		.367
Three 9s or better			.476
Three Deuces or better			1.000
Aces-up or better	.167	.226	
Kings-up or better	.200	.356	
Queens-up or better	.242	.472	
Jacks-up or better	.283	.577	
10s-up or better		.670	
9s-up or better		.751	
3s-up or better		1.000	
Pair of Aces or better	.474		
Pair of Kings or better	.618		
Pair of Queens or better	.809		
Pair of Jacks or better	1.000		

*The opener should stand pat on the hand A,A,K,x,x.

64

to the purist, they have little practical value for the poker player out to make money.

Player B—criteria for betting. When B draws one card to his four flush, nine other cards are available that will make the flush. We have already seen that B should use a bluff ratio of 1:2. Player B should bluff on four and one-half cards that leave B with a busted four flush.

Each of the three lowest cards of the possible flush has three other mates in the deck, there are nine possible cards for pairing. By a nice coincidence, because of the structure of the poker deck, this probability is exactly the same as drawing the fifth card to complete the flush. Player B must apply this rule only half the time, however. By another useful coincidence, the suits of the poker deck are red and black, and the probability of drawing one or the other is .5. This gives us the following betting rules for Player B:

If B has made his flush, he bets.

If B has a black four flush and has paired one of his three lowest cards, he bets.

For example, Player B draws to the hand A, 10, 9, 5 of spades and catches the 9 of diamonds. According to our rule B should now make a bet the size of the pot.

It makes no difference if the criterion B uses is applied to a red four flush or a black four flush, it is only important to have a correct betting criterion and to stick to it.

The opener raises. We have not yet exhausted all the possibilities of the contest of the Opener versus the Four Flusher.

At the beginning of round 2, Player A, the opener, passes to Player B. Player B then bets the size of the pot, $12. Player A calls the bet with the top 50 percent of his hands. When should Player A come roaring back with a $36 raise, and when should Player B call the raise?

We have already given the criteria for Player A's calling hands. These criteria depend only upon the number of cards that Player A draws so that Player B will have no advance knowledge of whether Player A will call or not. Having called Player A now becomes the aggressor: He has the opportunity of coming out with a raise. In our example we have decided that the best hand Player B could have is a flush, so that if A has a full house or better, the hand clearly warrants a raise.

Player A can now borrow B's optimal strategy by using the 1:2 bluff ratio. For every two high hands Player A draws —a full house or better—Player A bets one bluff hand that could not even beat a straight. Player B should then replicate A's optimal defensive strategy. When faced with a $72 pot, the pot after Player A has called B's $12 bet and raised him $36, Player B should call with the top 50 percent of his flush hands.

However, the chances that Player A will draw a full house are slim. In the most common case, when Player A draws three cards, his chance of hitting a full house are about 1 in 80. The bluff raise is warranted, therefore, only once every 160 times. To spend any further time on this rare event would be a bit precious. For now, we are emphasizing the ideas behind the optimal strategy, not the explicit rules for esoteric cases. The bread-and-butter play, opener versus four flush, will arise often and in different guises.

The opener stands pat (poverty bluff). We have worked out the correct strategy for B's betting, noting that B should bluff with the same frequency regardless of how many cards A draws. In practice what happens? Very few players have an ironclad rule to tell them when to bluff, a rule that depends completely upon their own cards. Most players use a far more subjective method, a method that is usually influenced by the number of cards that the opener draws. Most players in B's position will bluff less frequently when A draws one card than when A draws three cards. If A draws only one card, A must have at least two pair. It is usually less inviting to try to bluff a player when he has two pair than when he has only one pair. However, some players will bluff more frequently when A draws only one card, figuring that A will think B surely must know that he can't be bluffed out with his two pair, thus B can't be bluffing, so A folds. At this point the reasoning starts going around in a vicious circle. The folly in the above subjective argument is that B's best strategy is simply to ignore the number of cards that A draws. The bluff ratio must depend only upon the ratio of B's bet to the size of the pot.

Suppose that A draws no cards and then passes to B. If A has a pat hand, anything from a straight through a full house, B is in trouble. Should B bet even if he has made his flush?

Table 3.3 gives the distribution of possible pat hands. There are several interesting facts to be noted: The probability that A has a flush or better is .466 (almost 1 out of 2); the probability that A has a full house or better is .199, (almost 1 out of 5). If B has made the blunder of coming in with a four straight, his position is almost hopeless. The chances of having the best hand with, say, an Ace-King-high flush are not bad, but they do not justify betting and facing a raise at pot limit poker. If B is certain that A has a pat hand and is not false carding, then B has no bet. However, can B be certain of A's hand just because A stood pat? Couldn't A be false carding, trying to intimidate B by standing pat on a pair?

Table 3.3

The Opener Stands Pat; Distribution of Pat Hands*

Hands	Probability
Straight flush	.002
9-high full house or better	.093
Full house or better	.199
Ace-high flush or better	.302
King-high flush or better	.371
Queen-high flush or better	.415
Jack-high flush or better	.440
Flush or better	.466
Ace-high straight or better	.519
Queen-high straight or better	.626
10-high straight or better	.732
8-high straight or better	.834
5-high straight or better	1.000

*The opener should also stand pat on the hands A,A,K,x,x. Using these rules, the opener is false-carding about 50 percent of the time he stands pat.

This play of standing pat on a pair against a potential flush has been a profitable play for me. The essential idea is to scare B out of bluffing. Most players will bet if they make their flush, but it takes a really intrepid player to try to bluff against a pat hand. Against the average player who does not have an automatic bluffing rule, A's standing pat is enough to stop any bluffing. Once B's confidence for bluffing is shaken, Player A's worries are over.

This play of the opener who stands pat on some hand less than a straight is called the *poverty bluff.* It has the frightening effect of a big bet without the opener having to put out any money. However, the cost of standing pat for A is that he loses his chance to make a full house. Any false carding should therefore be done with one-pair hands where the chance of making a full house is fairly remote.

From A's point of view there is another value in false carding: By false carding some of the time, A will conceal the times when he has a very strong hand. However, A cannot afford to stand pat on all of his one-pair hands, as there is no guarantee that B, refusing to be bullied, will not bet as before.

Player A should stand pat when:

He has a straight or better.

He has a pair of Aces and one of the side cards is a King.

When A stands pat, A will automatically pass to B on the second round. If B bets the size of the pot, A will call if he has a straight or better (50 percent of the time).

OPTIMAL STRATEGY AT A LIMIT GAME

We have gone through the reasoning for the optimal strategy when we are playing pot limit. In our example the pot contained $12 and Player B could bet the $12 pot. Does the optimal strategy for that situation apply to a non-pot-limit situation as well? If the answer is yes, can we discover the optimal strategy without going through a maze of tables and a labyrinth of mathematical arguments? The answer to these two questions is yes, there is a short cut to the optimal strategy.

The threat of a bluff determines A's calling strategy. However, Player A calls just frequently enough to neutralize the profit of B's bluffs. Calling more frequently would reward Player B too handsomely for the times that B has made his flush. **Player A calls with sufficient frequency so that Player B comes out exactly even on his bluffs.**

Let us relate this to pot limit. When B bets $12 to win a $12 pot, Player A should call half the time. Out of every two bluffs that B makes, one time A does not call and B wins $12; one time B is called by A and B loses $12. As a result, B comes out even on his bluffs.

Let us now apply our principle to a limit game. Again the pot contains $12, but the betting limit is $6. Player B may try to steal the pot with a modest bet, and Player A must call more frequently. When B bets half the pot, Player A must call B two-thirds of the time.

What happens when Player B bluffs? Out of every three $6 bluffs, one time Player A doesn't call and Player B wins the $12, and two times Player A calls and Player B loses $6 each time, for a total loss of $12. Out of the three bluffs, Player B comes out exactly even.

The key to Player B's strategy, the bettor's strategy, is the word guaranteed—maximum *guaranteed* profit.

Once B has made a bet Player A can always pass, holding Player A's calling profit to zero but at least not losing any money. But what happens when Player A calls? If Player B is not bluffing frequently enough, Player A will show an average net loss from calling. Splendid, but this profit is certainly not guaranteed because Player A need not call. On the other hand, if Player B is bluffing too frequently Player A is going to be making money by calling.

Player B bluffs with the precise frequency so that on the

average Player A comes out exactly even on his calls. Adopting the above criterion, Player B's profit is independent of whether or not—or how frequently—Player A calls.

Let us apply this working principle when the limit is $6, one-half the pot. Player B adopts the 1:3 bluff ratio. Out of every four bets, one bet is a bluff. Three times A runs into a flush, losing $6 a call for a total loss of $18, and one time A catches B bluffing for a win of $18 ($12 pot plus B's $6 bet). Player A comes out exactly even on his calls. Player A should call with the top two-thirds of his hands.

When the limit is $4, one-third the pot, Player B's bluff ratio should be 1:4. Similarly, Player A's calling percentage should be 75 percent, that is, Player A should call with the top 75 percent of his hand, holding B's profit to zero on his bluffs.

Expected Value

In this chapter we have developed an optimal strategy for the two players, the opener versus the caller with a four flush. We have shown that the four flusher can guarantee himself a certain portion of the $12 pot with this strategy, but so far we have sidestepped the question: Should Player B even be in the pot with his four flush?

The answer depends on how much it costs Player B to call on the first round. If it costs B more money to call on the first round than he can guarantee himself by his optimal strategy, then Player B is losing money by being in the pot.

We have computed that Player B can guarantee himself around $3.60 out of each $12 pot by using his optimal strategy in pot-limit poker. However, this computation disregarded two factors that now become important. First, Player A can be expected to come up with a full house about 44 times out of 1,000. Second, Player B makes his flush slightly less frequently than 1 time out of 5, namely 9 times out of 47. Taking these two considerations into account, the maximum guaranteed profit for Player B drops to exactly $2.98.

This profit for Player B is the *expected value* of his hand. Although we have used a $12 second-round pot in our examples, the strategy is clearly independent of the $12. The expected profit is simply a fixed percentage of the pot. In this particular case the percentage is 24.8 percent of the pot.

One final consideration needs to be stressed here. Suppose B has the four flush A, 10, 9, 5 of spades and catches another Ace in the draw to give him two Aces. Player B has some chance of coming up the winner, increasing the amount of money that B might win. The prospects of winning on two Aces raises the expected value 20 cents in a $12 pot. With an Ace-high four flush on the first round, the expected value of the hand rises to $3.18.

We can now decide when it is profitable for B to call on the first round. With an Ace-high four flush, it is profitable for B to call on the first round if the pot offers 3 to 1 odds. For example, if the ante is $6 and A opens for $3, B can profitably call for $3 with an Ace-high four flush. It is only costing B $3 to enter a $12 pot, and B's expected value is $3.18.

What is the expected value of a four flush in a limit game? Let us assume a limit of $6 in our $12 pot, half the pot. The four flush doesn't make quite as much money. When the limit is $6, the four flush now only makes an average of $2.81. If the limit is less than $6 the expected value drops even further. A four flush in limit poker is definitely less profitable than in a pot-limit or table-stakes game. In a limit game the four flush needs almost 4 to 1 odds to justify a first-round call.

It should be noted that the expected value of a hand is not the probability that the hand will be the best hand after the draw but a more sophisticated indicator of how much money the hand will win. For example, with a four flush the expected value is .249 of the pot, and the probability that the four flush will be the best hand after the draw is only .183.

The Opener versus the Four Straight

In the previous example we assumed that Player B was drawing to a four flush. Would it have made any difference if Player B had drawn to an open-ended four straight? For example, what if Player B had called on the first round and drawn to the hand 6,7,8,9, where not all the cards were of the same suit? Strategically not one bit of difference. Player A would be totally indifferent; he would use the same calling strategy. Player B, playing optimally, should also be using the same bluff: strength ratio.

However, before spelling out a new set of tactical rules for Player B, let us look at the bottom line, the expected value of the four straight—in this case, .22 of the pot. In a $12 pot, the four straight has an expected value of only $2.64 (.22 ×

$12). If the limit is half the pot, $6, the expected value drops to $2.60. Seldom does Player B get justifiable odds, and for this reason we shall not spell out strategic rules for playing a four straight. Rather, the basic rule is: **Never make a first round call on a four straight.**

Summary

The two most important elements of a poker strategy are a *bluff ratio* for attacking and a *calling percentage* for defense. The bluff ratio and the calling percentage depend upon the size of the bet. For example, if B bets half the pot, B should use a 1:3 bluff ratio and A should call with the top two-thirds of his hands. Tables 3.4 and 3.5 summarize the opener's strategy.

Table 3.4

Optimal Strategy for Player B, the Four Flusher

Player B Bets	Player B's Bluff Ratio	Bluff Hands
The pot	1:2	A black four flush where one of the three lowest cards is paired.
One-half the pot	1:3	Pairs the lowest card.
One-third the pot	1:4	A club four flush and one of the three lowest cards is paired.
Twice the pot	2:3	A four flush and one of the two lowest cards paired.

The battle plans for Player A (the opener) and Player B (the four flush) represent our strategy in its simplest form.

74

Player B is the aggressor, hoping to make his flush on the draw. But if he doesn't, B still has a fighting chance by bluffing. When B bets the pot his optimal strategy at pot limit is realized by using the 1:2 bluff ratio. That is, B makes one bluff for every two high hands he bets. Using this double-barrelled gun, B achieves his maximal attack.

Table 3.5

The Opener, Player A, versus the Four Flusher, Player B:
Second-Round Play

Player B Bets	Percentage of Times That A Calls	Player A Draws	Calling Hands
The pot	50	3 cards	Pair of Aces or better
		1 card	Queens-up or better
		2 cards	Three 9s or better
One-half the pot	67	3 cards	Pair of Kings
		1 card	10s-up or better
		2 cards	Three 7s or better
One-third the pot	75	3 cards	Pair of Queens with an Ace or King kicker or better
		1 card	9s-up or better
		2 cards	Three 5s or better

When B bets the pot A must defend, and A's optimal defense means calling the bet 50 percent of the time and calling with the best 50 percent of his hands.

The cut and thrust of the strategy continues, as now A can

threaten to become the aggressor by raising B. Certainly if A has a full house he should raise. Player A can also borrow a leaf from B's strategy by making a bluff raise, using the 1:2 bluff ratio.

CHAPTER 4

Basic
Second-Round
Strategy:
Two Players

Before ever sitting down to a night of poker, while still safely beyond the siren sounds of riffling cards and the tattoo of the chips, you should reflect on the game. You must devise a profitable strategy to use against the toughest players. In a tough game, stick to the rules we derive in this chapter. They may seem a bit bewildering at first but, as you will see, we derive them from the basic principles of optimal strategy.

The most common situation in second-round betting pits the opener against one caller who has not backed into the pot. Player A opens the pot in Position 4 and Player B, in Position 6, calls the bet. There are no other callers or first-round raises. In any night of poker this two-person, second-round donnybrook leads to long-term wins and losses.

The strategic elements of chapter 3—high-hand betting, frequency of bluffing and calling—combined now with *false carding,* provide the optimal strategies for A and B. False carding means deliberately not drawing the maximum number of cards necessary to improve your hand in order to conceal the weakness or strength of your hand. Example: The opener often draws only one card to a pair (hiding the weakness of the hand to prepare a bluff) or draws one card to trips (hiding the strength of the hand to prepare for a high-hand bet).

I remember a game in which a friend of mine Player A, opened the pot and was called by Player B. Player B had not previously passed. My friend, Player A, stood pat, and B drew three cards. On the second round A passed! Player B, of course, then passed.

Player A showed his straight and won the pot. Player B, a man who would rather be one-up than a winner, asked Player A if he were at all familiar with the rules of poker. "Perhaps he didn't realize," taunted B, "that a straight is a mighty powerful hand." Player A replied in a voice laden with rationality that once he had stood pat, he had given away the fact that he had at least a straight. If he had bet no one could have called with less than a straight. Furthermore, argued A, he might have been subjected to a raise if anyone caught a full house. Stunned silence hit the game, followed by laughter.

Player A later asked me whether his reasoning was wrong or the game was merely populated by Philistines. I tried to explain as gently as I could that when a player stands pat he does not necessarily have a straight or better. In fact, some larcenous players make quite a bit of money by standing pat on the most pathetic hands (called a pat bluff)—this is an example of false carding.

The moral of the story, or at least the moral that I favor,

is that unless a player has some method of false carding he will find himself losing valuable opportunities. Also, the false carding must be done systematically to protect a player from overdoing it. I have seen enough players who can be counted on to try a pat bluff every hour on the hour, trying to buy the title of "The Last of the Big Bluffers."

The optimal strategy provides a way to judge which weak hands merit standing pat and bluffing. If a player will meticulously follow the opening and calling rules given in chapter 2, he will neither lose much money nor find himself with small hands contemplating calling big bets. But not losing at poker could also be accomplished by simply not playing, plus gaining a good night's sleep as a bonus. In order to make money, a player must know all the subtleties of second-round betting—when a hand is either strong enough to bet or so weak that a bluff is in order, and when a hand qualifies for a good solid pass.

Opener's Strategy

It is a six-handed, Jacks-or-better game; the pot has been opened by Player A in Position 4 and called by Player B in Position 6. There are no other callers.

Before the draw Player B knows only that A has something between a pair of Jacks and a straight flush, but he also knows the distribution of these hands. Since Player A draws first, the draw may reveal something more about the hand. But Player A is no fool. He knows that his draw may furnish potentially damaging information so he tries to obliterate any valid information from his draw. Among expert players, A's standing pat will not necessarily mean that he holds a big hand.

What should Player A do? Whatever he finally does, he must plan for the second-round betting before he has drawn cards, because false carding in the draw must be part of later betting plans.

There are two quite different scenarios for Player A. First, if A stands pat or draws one card he is oozing strength, possibly false, and he is looking down the barrel at Player B, ready to blow him out of the pot with a big bet. Second, Player A draws three cards. Player A is now shamelessly admitting that he started with only a lonely pair and is putting his faith in the draw. Player A's opponents could hardly miss A's drawing three, and although A could improve, B knows what the chances for improvement are. So in this second case Player A should probably pass after drawing three cards. The possible exception is when Player B also draws three cards.

The situation when both Player A and B draw three cards is the most complicated and will be dealt with later in the chapter. The reason for the complications is that both A and B gave away the information that they have only one pair, and they both have seen eight cards (five cards before the draw and three additional cards in the draw). An expert player will put his mind to utilizing this additional information. It may seem counter-intuitive, but the more information available, the more complicated the optimal strategy must be in order to utilize the information. The text will take up the easier case first, when Players A and B do not both draw three cards.

BETTING STRATEGY

The opener, Player A, bluffs with a pair of Jacks or Queens. Player A might very well disguise the weakness of his hand by drawing one card or by standing pat and then betting. These tactics can catch Player B in a dilemma worthy of Hamlet, to call or not to call. The optimal defensive strategy, explained in chapter 3, can resolve this dilemma for Player B. If A bets the pot, B should call with the top half of his strength hands. The top half of B's hands (see tables 4.1 and 4.2) range from a pair of Aces with a Queen kicker to four Aces when B draws three cards, and from two pair Queens-up through a full house when B draws only one card.

What hands are sufficiently high for Player A to bet? To answer this question let us consider two cases:

Case 1: Suppose the caller, Player B, draws three cards and Player A bets the pot on the second round with two pair Queens-up. If Player B is playing correctly he will fold half the time. If he follows his optimal strategy he will fold with the bottom half of his hands. In these situations Player B has no better than a pair of aces, Queen-high, and so Player A has the best hand anyway. The bet accomplishes nothing.

Of the 1,000 times Player A makes the bet and the 500 hands when Player B calls it, Player A can expect the following (see table 4.1):

Player A loses 288 hands when B has at least Kings-up.

Player A wins 212 hands (500 − 288) when B calls with only a pair of Aces.

Player A has a net loss of 76 hands (288 − 212).

Table 4.1

**Hand Distribution of the Caller Drawing Three Cards to Either
a Pair of Aces or a Pair of Kings***

Callers Final Hand	Number of Hands (out of 1,000)
Full house or four of a kind	13
Three Aces or better	76
Three Kings or better	127
Two pair, Aces-up or better	224
Two pair, Kings-up or better	288
Pair of Aces, Queen-high or better†	500
Pair of Aces or better	725
Pair of Kings or better	1,000

*A pair of Kings that contains neither a Jack nor a Queen as a side card unless the hand also contains an Ace. A pair of Kings without these conditions does not qualify as a first-round calling hand.

†The medium hand is a pair of Aces that did not improve, but one of the side cards drawn in the second round is a Queen.

Queens-up definitely does not qualify as a betting hand for Player A. When Player B draws only one card (see table 4.2) Player A will do even worse, coming out with a net loss of 490 bets.

Case 2: Now suppose the caller draws three cards and Player A bets the pot on the second round with three deuces. In 1,000 games Player B's optimal strategy dictates folding 500 times with the bottom half of his hands. Again, Player A has the best hands anyway so nothing is gained by the bet.

Of the 500 hands, when Player B calls the bet he can expect the following (see table 4.1):

Player A loses 127 hands when Player B has made at least trip Kings.

Player A wins 373 hands (500 — 127) when Player B has not made trips.

Player A has a net profit of 246 (373 — 127).

When Player B draws only one card, Player A will do even better (see table 4.2). A loses the bet 122 times and wins the bet 380 times for a net profit of 256 bets.

TABLE 4.2

Hand Distribution of the Caller When Drawing One Card

Before the Draw	After the Draw	Out of 1,000 high hands
Two Pair	Full house or better	85
or	Straight or better	122
Ace-King, Ace-Queen, and	Aces-up or better	256
Ace-Jack high four flushes.	Kings-up or better	378
All four-straight flushes.	Queens-up or better*	489
	Jacks-up or better	590
	Two pairs or better	990
	Pair Aces or better	1000
	Busted four flush†	

*The medium high hand is two pair, Jacks- and tens-up, but the rule Queens-up or better for calling is sufficiently accurate.

†The optimal strategy requires a call with 50 percent of *high* strength hands. Busted four flushes are not *high* hands. The number of busted four flushes is exactly one-half the number of two-pair hands, Kings and 10s or better.

From these two cases we see that Queens-up will not qualify as a profitable high-betting hand in our particular situation, but trip Deuces or higher promise a long-term profit. Of course along with the high-hand bets there must be a proper mixture of bluffs to guarantee the long-term profit (see chapter 3).

Several other considerations should be given before we

can formulate Player A's final betting strategy.

Player A should not bet all of his high hands. First, if he always bets his high hands, then by passing Player A gives away the vital information that he holds a weak hand and becomes a prime target for bluffing. For example, if Player A has two pair, say 10s-up, he does not have a betting hand. Nevertheless, although A has a respectable chance of having the best hand after the draw, he will not welcome an opponent's bet.

Second, Player B might very well not be following the optimal strategy. Instead, he may be calling with most of his four flushes and he may even be calling with open-ended four straights. It is quite uncomfortable for Player A to be betting into these potentially high hands and possibly facing a raise by Player B.

There is one final but very important consideration for Player A's second-round bet. According to the conventional wisdom of poker, always draw one card to trips. Why? First, because by drawing two cards to trips you are giving away important information, not about how weak your hand is but how strong. Drawing two cards does not guarantee trips, as you might be drawing two cards to a pair of Jacks to obfuscate. However, if you draw two cards and come out betting, you are putting an upper limit on your hand. The odds are only 2 out of 19 that you have anything better than trips (the odds that trips will improve to a full house or better when drawing two cards). Thus, you are vulnerable to raises by an opponent making trip Kings, Aces, or a flush.

We should accept the dictum of drawing only one card to trips for another reason as well. There are about 120,000 two-pair hands compared to about 55,000 trip hands possible on the first round. The odds therefore of having two pair compared to trips are about 2 to 1. If you draw one card to both two pair and trips, you come up with about 15,000 full houses. Consequently if now you bet your trips and full houses, the probability of having a full house when you bet becomes 1 in 4, rather than the 2 in 19 before, making an opponent's raise on high trips or a flush less inviting.

SELECTING BLUFF HANDS

The bluff hands for the opener are selected from first-round pairs of Jacks and Queens. There are 168,960 such one-pair hands, so criteria are needed that are easy to determine and easy to remember, criteria that will tell you when to stand pat or draw one card to these one-pair hands.

Let us determine a few simple criteria, seemingly capricious but quite easy to remember, that give the correct number of bluff hands. To this end we shall use the side cards; so when holding a pair of Jacks or Queens, the three side cards will tell you when to false card and prepare for a possible second-round bluff.

Stand pat when you hold:

1. A pair of Jacks or Queens when all of the cards in the hand are the same color and the hand does not contain an Ace. The hand "looks" like a flush.

2. A pair of Jacks or Queens of the same color when the side cards are of the opposite color and the hand does not contain an Ace or a King. The hand "looks" like a full

house. The exception is when one of the side cards is an Ace; then it is almost always preferable to draw three cards to the hand.

Criteria for drawing one card to a pair of Jacks or Queens. The bluff hands are selected from both the pair of Jack and pair of Queen hands; although a pair of Queens has a slightly greater potential in drawing, both sets of hands are used to randomize any information an opponent might get via his side cards. An opponent might well see a Jack, and if the opener used only pair of Jacks for bluff hands, then he would have a strong clue that the opener was not bluffing. By using both Jacks and Queens this "clue" becomes far less reliable—in other words, randomize the information.

Draw one card when you hold:

3. A Pair of Jacks when all the side cards are nine or less.

4. A Pair of Queens when all the side cards are eight or less.

These are poverty hands, indicating that the opponent has a pair of Aces or Kings. These hands (3 and 4) account for approximately 34,000 hands. For the rare hand satisfying both 1 or 2 and 3 or 4, stand pat on the hand.

If the opener needs a minimum of a pair of Queens to open and has a first-round caller, then the opener needs to substitute:

A pair of Queens both with 2 and 3 or 2 and 4 as side cards for criteria 1 and 2.

88

A pair of Queens when all the side cards are 10 or less for criteria 3 and 4.

Betting rules for the opener against one player, pot limit. Player A opens the pot in Position 4 in a six-handed game, Player B calls in Position 6. There are no other callers. Player A stands pat with a straight or better and all pairs of Jacks and Queens that satisfy criteria 1 and 2. Player A draws one card to all his trips, two-pair hands, and also to all pairs of Jacks or Queens that satisfy criteria 3 and 4.

Player A always bets the pot, $30, when:

He draws no card, with a straight or better, or with a pair of Jacks or Queens satisfying criteria 1 and 2.

He draws one card, with three 5s or better, or with all unimproved pairs of Jacks and Queens satisfying criteria 3 and 4.

See tables 4.3 and 4.4 for complete betting strategy. Note we have not taken the number of cards Player B draws into consideration. This is the correct strategy to follow unless the exceptional situation arises in which Player B stands pat or draws four cards.

If Player B folds, A wins; if he calls, A shows his hand and sees who wins. However, the battle enters a new phase if Player B calls A's $30 bet and raises $90.

The potential of A's bluff hand is ziltch when merely called. So when called and raised Player A should merely see how fast he can throw his bluff hands away.

Table 4.3

Hand Distribution of the Opener When He Stands Pat or Draws One Card at Pot Limit

	When A Stands Pat	
On First Round A Has	**On Second Round A Has**	**Out of 1,000 strength hands**
Pat hand, straight or better	Full house or better	197
Pair of Jacks or Queens*	Flush or better	465
	Straight or better	1000
	Pair Jacks or Queens	—

	When A Draws One Card	
On First Round A has	**On Second Round A Has**	**Out of 1,000 strength hands**
Three of kind, four of kind	Quads	10
Two pair	Full house or better	32
Pair of Jacks or Queens†	Three Aces, three Jacks, or better	174
	Three 10s, three 5s, or better	303
	Three 4s, three Deuces, or better	346
	Aces-up, Kings-up, or better	526
	Queens-up, 9s-up, or better	705
	10s-up, 9s-up, or better	839
	Two pair or better	1000
	Unimproved pair, Jacks or Queens	—

*A pair of Jacks (or Queens) when the Jacks (or Queens) are of the same color and all the side cards are of the same color.

†A pair of Jacks when all the side cards are nine or less, and a pair of Queens when all the side cards are eight or less.

Table 4.4

**Basic One-Card Strategy for the Opener,
Jacks or Better Against One Caller***

Player A's Hands on the First Round to Which He Draws One Card	Player A's Hand on the Second Round	Player A Will	Player B Raises, Player A Will	Player B Bets, Player A Will
Trips, quads	Quads through trip Queens	Bet	Call**	
Two pair	Trip Jacks to trip 5s	Bet	Fold	
Pair of Jacks†	Trip 4s to Queens-up	Pass		Call
Pair of Queens†	Jacks-up to 3s-up	Pass		Fold
	Unimproved pair, Jacks or Queens	Bet	Fold	

*This assumes that there is only one first-round caller, Player B; and he is an active caller. The strategy is independent of the number of cards Player B draws.

†A pair of Jacks when all the side cards are 9 or less; a pair of Queens when all the side cards are 8 or less.

**Reraise only with Kings full or better.

Player A must therefore protect only his high-betting hands and, as we have seen, the optimal strategy calls for Player A to call with the top half of his high-betting hands. Converting this rule into concrete poker hands, **Player A calls the $90 raise when:**

He stood pat, Ace-high straight or better.

He drew one, trip Queens or better.

Note that in the first case, of the top 50 percent of Player A's hands at least 40 percent are full houses. In the second case, when Player A draws one card, the top 55 percent of his raise-calling hands are full houses or better. Thus, Player B should be claiming a full house at the very least.

The next step takes us to a reraise by Player A of $270. Player A's reraise should take into consideration how many cards Player B draws. For example, if Player B draws three cards to a pair of Kings or Aces and makes a full house, there is a very high chance that he has at least Kings-full. This action is exciting, but it is also quite rare.

Some examples might help to clarify how the second-round betting rules apply to actual play:

Example 1: On the first round you open the pot with the hand Q, Q, 8, 5, 2. You are "ante stealing," but unfortunately you are called; there is just one caller and he has not previously passed. You throw away one card for the draw, the lowest card, in this case the Deuce. There are three possibilities: (1) The most unlikely—but possible—event is that you catch a Queen in the draw, ending up with three Queens. You have a powerful hand and therefore bet the pot. (2) It is more likely that you catch either a 5 or 8, giving you two pair Queens-up. Now you have a nice middling hand, not strong enough to bet but too strong to try to bluff. It is an excellent hand with which to pass at the beginning of the second round. You hope that Player B also passes, giving you good prospects for winning the pot in a showdown. If Player B comes out with a bet, you call with Queens and nines or better (a bluff-catching hand) and fold with any smaller hand. (3) The most likely event is that the draw leaves you no stronger than you were. You end up with a lonely pair of

Queens, a poverty hand. Therefore, come roaring out with a bluff bet, hoping for the best.

Example 2: The situation is the same as before, but this time as the opener you have a strong hand—J, J, J, K, 2. In the draw throw away your highest side card, in this case the King; there is more chance that a Deuce is left in the deck than a King. (Remember there is a caller.) You draw one card and bet, no matter what card you catch. If you catch a Jack or a Deuce, hope for a raise. Without this, the hand is not worth a call of a raise the size of the pot. If the raise is less than the size of the pot, you have a call.

The opener should draw three cards to all one-pair hands not previously mentioned in table 4.3: namely, a pair of Jacks when all the side cards are 9 or less, or a pair of Queens when all side cards are 8 or less. The situation is quite different now. The opener is admitting that he has only one pair. He may improve in the draw, but he starts out weak. He knows that Player B starts out with either two pair or a four flush. Against two pair Player A could improve sufficiently to throw a bet into Player B. But against a four flush, Player A is in no position to bet. The chance of making a full house or better by drawing three cards is only about 1 in 80. The opener should pass. If Player B bets, Player A should call with the top half of his hands. Translating this into a betting rule: **When the opener draws three cards and Player B draws one card, the opener should pass. On the second round if Player B bets the pot, the opener should call with two Aces and a Queen kicker or better.**

For the moment we shall delay the discussion of the opener's strategy when both he and Player B draw three cards. As we mentioned, this situation is the most technically difficult.

Caller's Strategy

Actually Player B's second-round strategy is quite simple, provided he has carefully followed his optimal first-round strategy rules. These rules were constructed with the precision of a Swiss watch and, if observed, the hands almost play themselves.

Player B has assembled a tough set of defensive hands, consisting of two types: the three-card-draw hands, a pair of Aces or Kings, and the one-card-draw hands, consisting of all two pair and a carefully chosen mixture of four-straight flushes and four flushes.

The first rule for Player B to master is when to call a bet by Player A—the most common problem against a good opponent. **When Player A bets the pot, Player B calls with:**

A Pair of Aces, Queen-high or better, after drawing three cards.

Queens-up or better, after drawing one card.

If Player A passes, B can bet with Kings-up or better. The choice of bluff hands, in the case where Player B draws one card, is now obvious from the first round. Player B bluffs on all his busted four flushes. Thus the analogy to a Swiss watch. The four-flush hand called into play is exactly the optimal number of times needed to bluff. When you draw to a four-straight flush you don't want to miss, but even if it does, the busted hand can be used for bluffing. See table 4.5.

There must be another criterion for bluff hands when Player B draws three cards. For example, Player B draws

Table 4.5

Basic One-Card Strategy for Player B Against the Opener, with Only Two Players in the Second Round

Player B's Hands on the First Round to Which He Draws One Card	Player B's Hand on the Second Round	If Player A Bets B Will	If Player A Passes B Will
Two pair	Full house through straight	Call	Bet*
All four-straight flushes	Aces-up to Kings and 7s-up	Call	Bet†
All A-K,A-Q, A-J high four flushes	Kings & 6s-up, Queens-up	Call	Pass
	Jacks-up, 3s-up	Fold	Pass
	Busted four flush	Fold	Bet†

*When Player A passes, B bets and A raises, then Player B will call with two pair, Aces and Queens or better.

†If Player A draws two cards and passes, Player B should pass with anything less than a straight and bluff only on busted four straight flushes.

three cards, Player A draws one card, and Player A passes. Player A's drawing of one card and then passing signifies that he has at least a solid two pair, and he has no interest in initiating any bets. For Player B, any second round one-pair hand would serve as a bluff hand. Thus, Player B selects a bluff hand when he has seen as many high cards as possible.

We can now give Player B's strategy once Player A has passed. **When Player A passes, Player B bets the pot with:**

Two pair, Kings and 7s or better.

All busted four flushes, when Player B draws only one card.

A Pair of Aces, at least King-high, when Player B draws three cards.

Opener and caller both draw three cards: Strategies for Players A and B. The case in which both the opener and caller draw three cards is the most deceptive situation for second-round betting. The technical subtleties arise because both players have seen eight cards after the draw: five cards on the first round and three more on the second. An alert player following his optimal strategy must incorporate all of this information into his overall plan of action.

Player A has opened the pot on the first round in a seat where a pair of Jacks is a profitable opening hand. He has drawn three cards, marking him with a pair from Jacks to Aces. The minimal profitable calling hand is a pair of Kings, so the opener should assume that the caller has either a pair of Kings or Aces. The opener works out a strategy against a pair of Kings or Aces—that is also valid against any caller who comes in with "shorts"—any pair less than Kings.

Briefly, the second-round strategy consists of the following principles:

1. Any hand from Aces-up is a possible betting hand for the opener, from Kings-up for the caller.

2. Any hand from three Aces or better is a raising hand for either player.

3. The opener must save some of his good hands for sand-bagging.

4. The opener has far more than an adequate supply of

bluffs in the hands that consist of an unimproved pair of Jacks or Queens.

Kings-up is not a good hand for Player A to bet. If A holds a pair of Kings, the odds are 6 to 1 that B started out with a pair of Aces; there is too great a chance now of B's having the best hand for A to initiate a bet. But, if A has Aces-up, the odds are 6 to 1 that B started out with a pair of Kings. In this case Player A has a relatively safe bet. (There are six different pairs of Kings that can be selected from four Kings but only one pair of Aces that can be chosen from two Aces.) Aces-up runs only a small risk of running into a raise. The simplest rule that A can use for betting high hands is to bet only if he started out with a pair of Aces that improved on the draw, but because he must save some hands for sandbagging, he should not bet all of these hands.

Some consideration should be given to bluff hands. In particular it is quite important for A that B not be able to tell from his own cards when A is bluffing. If A only bets with Aces-up or three Aces, the object of A's strategy is to attack when B starts out with a pair of Kings. But what corresponding bluff hands will probably find B with a pair of Kings? These are the hands when A holds an unimproved pair of Jacks or Queens and two of the side cards are Aces.

When Player A opens on a pair of Jacks or Queens he is ante stealing. With about one-fourth of these ante stealers, he false cards and tries to steal the pot with a bet. However, when Player A draws three cards to these pairs and fails to improve his hand—assuming the hand is not a bluff hand, that is, not having seen two Aces—the best philosophy is to abandon any hope of winning the pot. Player A should only try to avoid being bluffed too frequently when he starts out with a pair of Kings or Aces and draws three cards. So the block of hands that Player A will defend starts with a pair of Aces or better after he draws three cards and sees Player B do the same. See table 4.6.

Table 4.6

Player A's Second-Round Betting Strategy: Players A and B Both Draw Three Cards

Player A Bets the Pot With:	If Player B Calls and Raises the Pot, Player A Calls With:
Improved pair of Aces* or pair of Jacks or Queens, having seen two Aces.	Two pair, Aces and Queens, or better.
Player A Passes With:	Once Player B Has Bet Player A Calls With:
All hands not mentioned in the first column.	A pair of Aces, Queen-high, or better. Player A would raise with trip Aces or better.

*Player A starts with pair of Aces, each Ace of a different color, and improves to at least Aces-up.

Example: A typical bluff hand would be JS, JC, AS, 4D, 5D on the first round, and after drawing three cards to the pair of Jacks, the hand ends up JS, JC, AH, 9H, 7D. Player A still has a lonely pair of Jacks but has seen two Aces, making the odds 6 to 1 that Player B started out with a pair of Kings. The hand becomes an excellent bluff hand.

If Player B calls the bet and raises the size of the pot, Player A calls with Aces and Queens, or better.

To finish off the second-round strategy for Player A see table 4.6.

Let us now turn to Player B's strategy when both Player A and B draw three cards. When Player A comes out with a bet the size of the pot Player B calls with the top half of his hands. As we see from table 4.1, the midhand is a pair

98

of Aces, Queen-high. This is straightforward play by the book. The case is more interesting when Player A passes. Any improved pair of Kings or better, that is, Kings-up or better, will be high-betting hands, and the lowest pair of Kings will furnish the bluff hands. See table 4.7.

Table 4.7

Player B's Second-Round Betting Strategy: Players A and B Both Draw Three Cards

If Player A Bets the Pot, Player B Calls With:	Player A Raises the Size of Pot With:
Pair of Aces, Queen-high, or better	Trip Aces or better* Pair of Aces, having seen two Kings
If Player A Passes, Player B Bets the Pot With:	*If Player A Calls and Raises, Then Player B Calls With:*
Two pair, Kings and 7s, or better	Two pair, Aces and Queens, or better

*Trip Kings, having seen one Ace, is also a raising hand.

Player B bets with:

Kings-up or better.

Pair of Kings where all the side cards are 10 or less, having seen an Ace on the first round.

Example: Player B calls on the first round with K, K, 2, 7, A, throws away the three odd cards, and ends up with K, K, 3, 8, 10. A bluff bet is now in order. The bluff is aimed at the times Player A has improved his pair of Jacks or Queens in the draw or has a pair of Kings or Aces.

Deviations from the Optimal Strategy

The optimal strategies for Players A and B have been given for the two-man situation in which there is no first-round raise. But what should you do when your opponent deviates from his optimal strategy?

To answer this question we must first know how we can be certain that he is deviating. If he bets too light a hand or passes on too big a hand (unfortunately, something that you cannot know until the hand is over), following your optimal strategy would automatically return its own reward. However, if you are certain that an opponent is deviating from his optimal strategy, either by consistent bad play or incorrect draws, then you can take certain measures to increase your winnings.

Let us concentrate on the situation in which your opponent draws two cards, there are only two players, and there have been no first-round raises.

Player B's two-card draw seems to imply that he is drawing to trips, but his failure to raise on the first round indicates that he is pulling to a pair, holding a kicker. Player A should not take the threat of trips too seriously.

When Player A draws one card or stands pat, his betting strategy should be exactly as before (see table 4.4). Here Player A is only making his high bets on at least medium-sized trips, so Player B's two-card draw is only a small threat.

When Player A draws three cards and Player B draws two cards, Player A should automatically pass to Player B. Player A should drop into this defensive stance because the possibility of B's holding trips is now more of a threat. It would be foolhardy of Player A to bet his high two pair against Player B's possible trips. Also, if Player B voluntarily lowers his drawing potential by drawing only two cards to a pair, Player A's pass is justified. In either case, a pass is justified. If Player B then comes out with a bet, Player A should call with the top half of his hands and he should raise with trip Jacks or better. Essentially Player A regards the situation as a three-card draw versus three-card draw, except that A should raise with slightly lower trips than he would have if Player B had actually made a three-card draw.

Adapting the strategy for anything opens. When passing from Jacks or better to anything opens, there is only one major change in the opening and one-card draw strategies. Namely, **Player A should open with all Ace-high four flushes and all four-straight flushes.** The one-card betting strategy now takes a form as before (table 4.8).

In a Jacks-or-better game, the opener has to turn a good many of his pairs of Jacks and Queens into bluff hands. To these hands, the opener draws only one card and comes out betting whether or not the hand improves. Drawing only one card, as the strategy dictates, is a conspicuous but unavoidable waste of the hand's potential.

In an anything-opens game, a limited number of four flushes offer much better possible bluff hands. A four flush has a much greater chance of becoming a high-betting hand by drawing one card (9 in 47) than a pair of Jacks does by drawing one card (2 in 47). Also, a flush is a much more comforting hand to have than trip Jacks. The rules for selecting these four flushes give the correct number of bluff hands called for by the optimal strategy. The opener should definitely limit himself to these bluff hands.

The pat hand and three-card-draw opening strategies re-

101

Table 4.8

*One-Card Strategy for the Opener at Anything Opens**

Player A's First-Round Hands	Player A's Second-Round Hands	Player A Will	Player B Raises, Player A Will	Player B Bets, Player A Will
Trips	Quads through trip Queens	Bet	Call	
Two pair	Trip Jacks through trip 5s	Bet	Fold	
Ace-high and four-straight flushes	Trip 4s through Queens-up	Pass		Call
	Jacks-up through 3s-up	Pass		Fold
	Busted four flushes	Bet	Fold	

*This strategy is based on the assumption that the game is pot limit but is independent of the number of cards Player B draws.

main exactly the same in anything opens as in Jacks or better to open.

Problems

It is assumed that you have mastered the optimal strategy for the following situations and now have a chance to apply your knowledge to the game. Your opponent may or may not be playing his optimal strategy, but until his actions tell you otherwise, it is always safer to assume that he is playing an optimal strategy. In all of these problems there are only two players at the end of the first round of betting. It is a seven-handed game. Player A sitting in Position 4, Player B sitting in Position 6; there were no first-round raises. For the first ten problems you are Player A, the opener.

Problem 1: You are Player A. On the first round you have JS, JH, 3C, QH, KC. You discard the three side cards and after the draw your hand is JS, JH, 2C, 4D, 4C. Player B draws four cards! How do you start off the second-round betting?

Answer: Muggins Law. Player B has drawn four cards, presumably to an Ace, against an opponent who has at least a pair of Jacks. You have a genuine Muggins in your game. The Law of Muggins is: Let the damn fool take long odds, just make the payoff small. Player B called your opening bet and drew four cards, with only a .25 probability of having a pair of Aces or better.

So pass. Player B has a surplus of bad hands, possibly he will bluff or bet his pair of Aces. If B bets, you should call, not raise. Incidently if you lose, it would be poor form to complain.

Problem 2: You are Player A. On the first round you have the hand JS, JC, AS, 3C, 4C. How many cards do you draw?

Answer: With any pair holding an Ace kicker it is always preferable to draw three cards to the pair. There is a good chance that if Player B has a pair, it is not a pair of Aces. Therefore even if your hand does not improve in the draw

103

but catches another Ace, you have a good chance of stealing the pot by bluffing.

Problem 3: You are Player A holding JH, JC, 9H, 7C, 3S. The optimal strategy tells you to throw the smallest card, the 3S, and to draw only one card. If you are only masking your hand by drawing one card, why throw the smallest card?

Answer: Throwing the smallest card is preferable to throwing any of the other side cards in two cases: when the opponent holds Jacks and 9s or when he holds Jacks and 8s or 7s. In the first case you might hit a 9 in the draw, giving you Jacks and 9s with a 7 as the side card. He may draw a card less than a 7, showing the advantage of throwing the 3 rather than the 7. In the other case, if you had thrown the 9 you would have had no chance to beat the opponent. Admittedly these cases are rare, but there is absolutely no cost to this play, and there is some chance for gain.

Problem 4: You are Player A. On the first round, you have the hand QH, QS, AS, 3C, 4C. You discard the three side cards and come up with QH, QS, 5D, 5H, 8D after the draw. Player B draws three cards. How do you play the second round?

Answer: This is an ideal bluff-catching hand. Your having the Ace on the first round indicates that Player B started out with a pair of Kings, unless he is a loose player. So he may very well try a bluff if his hand does not improve. You have a nice medium hand, too strong for a bluff and too weak to bet. Pass. If Player B comes out with a bet, call him.

Problem 5: You are Player A holding JH, JS, 5C, 5S, 4C. You draw one card to your two pair and catch a 3D. Player B draws three cards. On the second round you pass and Player B bets the pot. What do you do?

Answer: Your hand is just a bit too weak to call the bet; you should fold. If the bet had been two-thirds or half the pot, a call would have been in order. Incidentally, all of your side cards were low, indicating that Player B might well have had a strong hand.

Problem 6: You are Player A. In the first round you have 4S, 4H, 4C, 10H, AC. You throw the AC and draw one card, a 2D. Player B draws three cards. How do you play the second round?

Answer: As Player B called your opening there is less likelihood of an Ace being in the deck than a Deuce. Since an opponent cannot simultaneously hold trip fours, the kicker is irrelevant. So in drawing one card to trips, masking the strength of the hand, always throw the highest side card. You have laid a nice trap for your opponent. You would like to see one more bet go in the pot, but no second-round raise. So pass and hope that your opponent does your betting for you.

Problem 7: You are Player A. On the first round you have QS, QH, 8H, 8D, 4C. You discard the 4C and catch a Deuce. Player B draws two cards. At the beginning of the second round you pass and Player B bets the pot. What do you do?

Answer: What you are holding is in the top half of your passing hands and there is no reason not to call. Your opponent has just made a tactical error. The two-card draw of

Player B signifies nothing. In Position 6 he would make far more by a first-round raise on trips than by just calling. This is an excellent chance for a bluff by Player B.

Problem 8: You are Player A. On the first round you have the hand AS, AH, KD, 8H, 7C. How many cards should you draw?

Answer: The answer depends on how many cards you estimate Player B will draw. If Player B is going to draw three cards to a pair of Aces or Kings, then the correct draw for you is two cards. If Player B has a pair of Aces, the King kicker would give you a big edge, and if Player B has only a pair of Kings, little is lost. When Player B draws only one card by keeping the King you are only lowering your chances of improving the hand, with no compensation.

Your possession of the two Aces and one King makes it far more likely that Player B's first round hand is two pair and not a pair of Aces. Thus the correct answer is that you should draw three cards.

A less than ethical player in your position will often try a *balk,* that is, he will try to lure Player B into giving away his draw. For example, you might slowly throw one or two cards away but not tell the dealer how many cards you are going to draw, watching B's reaction to see if B will act out of turn. Then you determine your draw by how many cards Player B discards. If Player B discards three cards, clearly you should draw only two cards. I would not suggest such shady tactics, but watch for it in your opponents. Usually these ploys just slow up the game and come to naught against alert opponents.

Problem 9: You are Player A. On the first round you hold the hand JS, JH, 2S, 6S, 10S (a combination four flush and pair of Jacks). How many cards do you draw? Do you draw to the pair or the four flush?

Answer: You should split your pair of Jacks and go for the flush, even if you must announce this action. (For the proper second-round strategy, see chapter 3.) Some local ground rules come into play here when the opener "splits his openers." In some games the opener must announce that he is splitting his openers when he draws, show the opponents his discard—in this case the Jack of hearts—and after the hand is over show the other Jack.

In other games when the opener draws only one card, he puts the discard to the side, without announcing what he is doing. Then after the hand is over he must show that his hand plus the discard gave him a proper opening for Jacks or better. The latter rule usually prevails in home games, but certainly inquire about this rule before playing.

Problem 10: You are Player A. On the first round you hold the hand AS, AH, 2S, 6S, 10S. How many cards do you draw?

Answer: This is the same situation as the previous problem, with Aces substituted for Jacks. Against one opponent, you should keep the pair of Aces and draw three cards. A pair of Aces is too strong a hand to abandon. With Jacks or Queens you were definitely beaten, so you split the pair. With Kings it is a borderline case but the strategy favors keeping the Kings. Side cards might help a decision here.

For the remaining ten problems, you will become Player B, the first caller. The ante again is $10 and you are sitting in a seven-handed, Jacks-or-better game. Your hand is presented and you are asked to solve certain poker situations. The format of the problems is slightly altered now to provide relevant information at a glance in tabular form—not unlike the usual bridge-problem presentation.

Problem 11: You are now Player B. Your hand before the draw AH, KH, 8H, 7H, 6D. Your hand after the draw is AH, KH, 8H, 7H, AD.

Player	A	B
Position	4	5
First Round	$10 open	$10 call
Draw	Three cards	One card
Second Round	Pass	?

What should you, Player B, do in the second round after Player A has passed?

Answer: You start off with a hand that will either be a high betting hand or, if you miss your flush, a bluff hand. Although you have missed your flush, you have come with a nice middle-class hand, a pair of Aces. The hand has a good chance of winning the pot, but not enough chance to risk any more bets on the hands; that is, it is neither a high-betting hand nor a bluff hand. Therefore, Player B should pass, show the hand down.

Problem 12: You are Player B. Your hand before the draw KS, KH, 3S, 4S, 9S.

Player	A	B
Position	5	7
First Round	$10 open	$10 call
Draw	Three cards	?

108

Should you, Player B, draw three cards to your pair of Kings or one card to your four flush?

Answer: You should draw three cards to your pair of Kings after you see that Player A has drawn three cards. There is a good chance that you can win the pot with a pair of Kings, once you know that A is drawing to a pair. If Player A draws only one card or if you had been overcalled by a third player, then you should go for the flush by throwing the KH.

Problem 13: You are Player B. Your first round hand is AS, AD, KD, 10D, 3C.

Player	A	B
Position	3	5
First Round	$10 open	$10 call
Draw	Three cards	?

How many cards should you draw: three cards to your pair of Aces or two cards to AS, AD, KD?

Answer: If you draw two cards you will give away your hand to an alert opponent, dispelling all doubt of whether you have a pair of Aces or Kings, thereby limiting any second-round action. By drawing three cards, there would still be some mystery about your hand. The correct procedure then depends on whether you wish to insure your winning the $30 pot, or gamble on winning a bigger pot.

Usually you should draw three cards. Exceptions would be when you are playing in a limit game where subsequent winnings are minimal, or when Player A is known to be a very conservative player who wouldn't open on a pair of Jacks or Queens.

Problem 14: You are Player B. Your hand before the draw is 3S, 4S, 5S, 6S, AH. Your hand after the draw is 3S, 4S, 5S, 6S, 9H.

Player	A	B
Position	6	7
First Round	$10 open	$10 call
Draw	One card	One card
Second Round	Pass	?

What should you, Player B, do on the second round after Player A has passed to him?

Answer: You should come out with a bet the size of the pot. The four flushes that you chose to call with on the first round are translated into betting hands, either a bluff or a high-hand bet.

A tactical point should be mentioned here. If you play the optimal strategy, you know that you will bet the hand no matter what card you catch in the draw once Player A has passed. Thus there is a tendency to bet the hand without looking at the draw. This is quite all right, provided that the opposition does not notice your action. At least pretend to look at your draw before you take any action.

Problem 15: You are Player B. Your hand before the draw is KC, KD, 2S, 7H, AC. Your hand after the draw is KC, KD, 8H, 8D, 6C.

Player	A	B
Position	6	7
First Round	$10 open	$10 call
Draw	Three cards	Three cards
Second Round	Pass	?

What should you Player B do on the second round after Player A has passed?

Answer: You should bet the pot. This is a classic high-betting hand against a three-card draw.

Problem 16: You are Player B. Your hand before the draw is AS, AC, 6D, 6H, 4D. Your hand after the draw is AS, AC, 6D, 6H, 8C.

Player	A	B
Position	3	5
First Round	$10 open	$10 call
Draw	Two cards	One card
Second Round	Pass	?

How should you, Player B, play your Aces-up after Player A has passed?

Answer: The answer depends on what type of hand you think Player A has on the first round. Does he have trips? Possibly small trips since he passed on the second round, or a pair of Jacks with an Ace kicker. In the first case it would be foolish to bet your Aces-up into trips. In the second case, with a pair of Jacks with an Ace kicker, there is very small chance of Player A calling if he did not improve his hand. A bet here would be equally fruitless. The deciding factor would be your having seen two Aces, making it less likely that Player A started out with a pair of Aces or a pair of Jacks with an Ace kicker.

You should pass, turn your hand over, and see who wins the pot.

The answer may seem a bit timid, but a dry twig breaking a mile away is about all the warning you get at the poker table.

Problem 17: You are Player B. Your hand before the draw is AS, AH, 2S, 4C, 5D. Your hand after the draw is AS, AH, AD, JD, 10C.

Player	A	B
Position	3	7
First Round	$10 open	$10 call
Draw	One card	Three cards
Second Round	$30	?

How should you, Player B, play the second round after Player A has started the round off with a $30 bet?

Answer: Trip Aces is certainly a strong hand, definitely strong enough to call Player A and hope to win the pot, but it is not strong enough to raise. When Player A is playing his optimal strategy, the top 27 percent of his high-betting hands are full houses or better. Hence, it is unprofitable to raise. It is far safer, profitably, only to call with trip Aces. In a limit game, a raise would probably be in order.

Problem 18: You are Player B. Your hand before the draw is AH, AC, 4H, JS, QS. Your hand after the draw is AH, AC, AD, 3C, 9S.

Player	A	B
Position	3	7
First Round	$10 open	$10 call
Draw	Two cards	Three cards
Second Round	$30	?

How should you, Player B, play your trip Aces on the second round after Player A has bet into you?

Answer: There is no doubt that you have to call the bet,

but should you raise? In problem 17, when Player A drew only one card, the answer was that you should only call, not raise. The difference here is that Player A drew two cards instead of one. By drawing two cards Player A has implied that he started with trips, at least on the first round, and wants the pot. Against an opponent starting with trips, three Aces is a jumbo hand, and you should have no hesitation about not only calling but throwing in a $90 raise.

Against this two-card pull you should raise.

Problem 19: You are Player B. Your hand before the draw is AS, AC, 7S, 6D, 2C. Your hand after the draw is AS, AC, KH, 6H, 8C.

Player	A	B
Position	5	6
First Round	$10 open	$10 call
Draw	Pat	Three cards
Second Round	$30	?

What should you, Player B, do after Player A stands pat and then comes out betting on the second round?

Answer: You are within the top half of your three-card-draw hands, so the optimal strategy dictates a call. This is always a tough decision, but unless you are thoroughly convinced by previous consistantly tight play by Player A—that is, Player A seldom or never bluffs—a call is in order.

Problem 20: You are Player B. Your hand before the draw is 3S, 4S, 6S, 7S, JD. Your hand after the draw is 3S, 4S, 6S, 7S, KS.

113

Player	A	B
Position	3	7
First Round	$10 open	$10 call
Draw	Pat	One card
Second Round	$30 bet	?

What should you, Player B, do on the second round with your King-high flush after Player A stood pat and bet the pot?

Answer: Clearly a call is in order, but you have more than a bluff-catching hand, you have a flush. So should you raise? The flush is only average, K high. The high-hand raising range starts with full houses. (The top 20 percent of Player A's true pat hands are full houses.) Thus, only a flat call is in order. Player B is the favorite to win the hand, even if A isn't bluffing, but B isn't strong enough to raise. (See table 3.3 for a distribution of pat hands.)

CHAPTER 5

First-Round Raise

A poker player dreams about picking up a full house, Aces-high against an opponent holding Kings-full. In novels the players may hold even bigger hands. These are the exotic hands that make poker exciting. They move fortunes from one side of the table to the other. Unfortunately, these hands do not occur frequently enough to keep the game at such fever pitch. And when they do, a good player will show remarkable restraint in contributing his money to an opponent holding a big hand.

Jumbo pots cannot be left to the luck of the draw. They must be built carefully by the most adroit manipulation of the first-round raise. Here, too, bluffing is most successful. Big hands mean first-round raises and reraises, but few people understand the proper play of the first-round raise. Poker folklore gives the totally misleading information that a player with two pair should raise the opener. If this absurdity is accepted, a whole carload of myths is then piled on top of such foolishness. To protect ourselves from such nonsense, let us stand back from the poker table, become detached kibitzers, and see what general principles we can deduce. On what hands, for example, should a player make a first-round raise? On what hands should the opener call or reraise?

Strategy for the Opener

Consider the usual poker situation: The ante is $10, Player A opens the pot for $10. Player B calls the $10 bet and raises $30.

In the beginning of play the pot contains $10, Player A comes on virgin land and stakes a claim for $10. Suddenly, an aggressive invader appears on the scene who will not content himself with merely calling Player A's bet and settling down to a nice gentlemanly second-round joust for a fairly small pot. Player B wants the pot immediately so Player B raises, resorting to terror tactics. Player A is forced to make a tough decision on the first round. If he stays in the game, he must consider the possibility of looking down the barrel of a possible $90 bet on the second round.

Without peeking at B's hand, who knows what hand the raiser could hold? Player A, the opener, certainly can't know. All Player A knows for certain is that Player B is betting $40 (his $10 call plus a $30 raise) to win a $20 pot (the $10 ante plus Player A's $10 opening bet). Player B could be bluffing and if so Player A would like to defend his interest in the pot. A good opponent certainly will use the terror tactics of bluff raising to great advantage, but Player A should certainly treat the situation with great caution. By using only what he knows, namely his own hand's contents and the fact that Player B bets $40 to win $20, Player A can come up with the correct strategy. He can apply the reasoning of the optimal strategy to devise the best course of play.

To stop Player B from profiting by first-round raising on his worthless hands, Player A should call B's raise one-third of the time: Two out of three times Player B wins $20, and one out of three times Player A calls the bluff so that Player B loses $40—Player B's profit is zero.

The game is far from over, however. In general Player B has the offensive. He declares that he has a big hand and that, if he knows what's good for him, Player A should pass at the beginning of the second round. If Player B makes a bet the size of the pot, now at $90, Player A should call this last bet one-half of the time.

Of course, Player A should call the first-round raise with the top one-third of his opening hands and call the second-round bet with the top one-half of his second-round calling hands. The following examples give a concrete calling strategy for use at the poker table.

Example 1: In a five-handed, Jacks-or-better game where the ante is $10, Player A, in Position 1, opens the pot for $10. All the players pass until it comes to Player B in Position 5, the dealer. Player B calls the $10 opening bet and raises $30. With what hands should Player A call?

The play has come down to two players, and Player A should call with the top one-third of his opening hands. To translate this rule into hands see table 5.1. Player A could

Table 5.1
Distribution of Opening First-Round Hands

Hands	Number of Hands	Percentage of all Opening Hands
Straight flush or better	40	.007
Four of a kind or better	664	.12
Full house or better	4,408	.8
Flush or better	9,516	1.8
Straight or better	19,716	3.7
Three Kings or better	28,164	5.3
Three 10s or better	40,836	7.6
Three 6s or better	57,732	10.8
Three Deuces or better	74,628	14.0
Aces-up or better	93,630	17.5
Kings-up or better	111,054	20.8
Queens-up or better	126,894	23.7
Jacks-up or better	141,150	26.4
Eights-up or better	174,414	32.5
Threes-up or better	198,180	37.0
Pair of Aces or better	282,660	52.7
Pair of Kings or better	376,140	68.5
Pair of Queens or better	451,620	84.2
Pair of Jacks or better	536,100	100.0

have opened with any one of 536,360 hands, that is, all hands with a pair of Jacks or better. One-third of 536,360 is 178,-787. The top one-third of the hands are all the hands with two pair, eights-up or better (174,414 hands). Therefore, the rule is: **Player A should call the raise with 8s-up or better.**

In many situations, however, the other players should not be ignored. For instance, a raiser is laying out money at long odds, and a third player, yet to act, may come in with a big hand to destroy the raiser.

Example 2: In a seven-handed, Jacks-or-better game where the ante is $10, Player A in Position 3 opens the pot for $10. Player B in Position 4 calls the $10 and raises $30. With what hands should Player A call?

There are two differences between Examples 1 and 2: First, a player in Position 3 in a seven-handed game should open only with a pair of Kings or better, not a pair of Jacks as before. Second, the players between the raiser and the opener cannot be ignored. The players in Positions 5, 6, 7, 1, and 2 must be considered potentially active callers; any of these players could have powerful hands. (In a seven-handed game, the players in Positions 1 and 2 should automatically pass in the first round.) The opener should consider all players between the raiser and the opener potential allies capable of preventing Player B from stealing the pot with a bluff. Even though all the players fold their hands after Player B has raised, Player A should shorten the probability of his call to one-fourth.

In terms of hands, there are 367,400 hands starting with a pair of Kings, and the top 92,000 hands range upward from two-pair Aces-up or better. Therefore, the rule is: Player A should call the raise with Aces-up or better.

Thus the calling rules differ somewhat depending on the situation. However, it is useful to develop rules that fit the game most of the time. Example 1 is more common than Example 2. The opener usually has a profitable opening hand that starts with a pair of Jacks, and generally there are not too many active callers between Players B and A.

The strategy from the opener's point of view is defensive. Player B is claiming a big hand or a big bluff, and Player A will try to defend his position as far as caution will allow. Player A's hands will generally range from two pair, 9s-up, to trip Aces. To all of these hands Player A should draw one card, giving away no information either how weak or how strong he is, and at the beginning of the second round Player A should pass (table 5.2 gives such a distribution.)

Table 5.2

Distribution of the Opener's Second-Round Hands
After the Raise*

Hands	Out of 1,000 Hands
Full house or quads	86
Trip Queens or better	166
Trip 9s or better	246
Trip Deuces or better	433
Aces-up or better	553
Kings-up or better	663
Queens-up or better	761
9s-up or better	1000

*After a first-round raise, Player A calls with all two pair, 9s-up or better, all trips, and all quads, and draws one card.

Before the draw the medium hand of the opener is about two pair, Kings-up. After the draw, the medium hand is two pair, Aces over tens. When raised, the general philosophy of the opener is to set up a strong defensive line. The opener should be a passive defender.

Of course if the opener has a pat hand, a straight or better, he cannot conceal the strength of his hand in the draw. He must stand pat in the draw, a fact that the raiser would not overlook. Therefore we can state the next general rule for the opener: **Player A should reraise on the first round with a straight or better and the proper number of bluff hands.** But more on the subject of a first-round reraise later.

Strategy for the Raiser

The player who raises the opener must realize that such terror tactics can backfire. The raiser has two problems: First, he is risking $40 to win only $20; second, he is facing a possible first-round reraise or a big second-round bet from the opener.

For these reasons the strength hands of the raiser must be strong indeed. Two-pair hands are too weak. As we can see in table 5.2 the medium hand for the opener after the draw is Aces over tens. The smallest strength raising hand must be trip Deuces. For planning a general raising strategy, we will take trip Deuces as the minimal strength raising hand.

To guarantee the raiser's profit on his strength hands, Player B should also use a fairly large number of bluff-raising hands. A first-round bluff raise is not an empty gesture; it is a good possibility. A bluff-raising hand should ideally have two qualities. First, it should not qualify for a profitable calling hand. To raise with such a profitable calling hand— a pair of Aces or two small pair—is conspicuous waste. Second, although the hand does not qualify as a calling hand, it should have some chance of improving to a big hand in the draw. Given these two criteria, it is apparent that four flushes admirably satisfy both conditions.

The exact number of bluff-raising hands can be computed, and the bluff-raising rule is: **Player B should make a first-round raise with all Ace-, King-, or Queen-high four flushes.**

Some Ace-high* four flushes were shown in chapter 4 to be profitably integrated into the calling strategy for Player B.

---

*Ace-high four flush, but not an Ace-King, Ace-Queen, Ace-Jack. These hands are profitably incorporated into the first-round calling hands.

Therefore we choose the next highest four flushes, unused until now, as raising hands.

Raising rule for Player B: Player B should raise on the first round with:

Trip Deuces or better (74,600 hands).

All Ace-, King-, or Queen-high four flushes (54,500 hands).

A hand that has a pair of Aces or Kings and a four flush is not a raising hand. With this hand it is preferable to call, not raise. This is a medium hand with interesting flexibility. Of course a four-card straight flush is too strong to bluff; it is a calling hand.

Table 5.3 gives the drawing rules and distributions for Player B at the beginning of the second round of betting.

To illustrate the effectiveness of this raising strategy we shall concentrate on the most usual situation. Player A opens the pot on the first round, Player B calls and raises the size of the pot. Player A merely calls the first-round raise. At the beginning of the second round Player A passes.

Player B should now take several possibilities into account before betting. The clue to each of them is how many cards the opener draws. In each case, Player B should tailor his strategy to include this information. There are three cases to consider.

Case 1: Player A draws one card. This is the optimal strategy for Player A. The analysis for Player B must be conducted by studying table 5.2 again. Player A could have called with anything starting at 9s-up, and after the draw he could hold anything from 9s-up through four Aces! Accord-

Table 5.3

Distribution of Player B's Raising Hands After the Draw

Hand Before the Draw	Hand After the Draw	Out of 1,000 Hands After the Draw
	Player B Draws One Card	
Quads or Trips	Full house or better	52
All King-high four flushes	Straight or better	138
All black Queen-high four flushes	Trip Aces, trip Queens, or better	261
	Trip Jacks, trip 9s, or better	384
	Trip 8s, trip Deuces, or better	677
	Busted King-high four flush	192
	Other busted four flushes	131
	Player B Stands Pat	
Straight or better	Full house or better	141
All red Queen-high four flushes	Flush or better	324
	Straight or better	667
	Busted red Queen-high four flushes	333

ing to table 5.2, Player A's medium hand is two pair, Aces and 10s. The top one-fifth of all Player A's hands run from trip 9s up, and this is a clue for Player B. Player B needs hands slightly better than the top one-fourth of Player A's for fear of a possible second-round raise. Therefore trip 9s or better are the second-round strength betting hands for Player B. We shall give the betting rules in table 5.4.

The bluff hands will come from those King-high four-flush hands that did not improve in the draw to flushes. These are bluff hands and satisfy the 2:1 bluff ratio required by the last round's optimal strategy.

All hands from trip Deuces to trip 8s should be passed. These are nice hands, with an excellent chance to win the pot, but they do not give good enough odds to invite a call and certainly not a raise.

Player B should pass with all busted Ace and black Queen-high four flushes after the draw. Do not try to bluff on these hands. If Player B tries to win the pot with a bluff on the first round and fails to improve these hands, he should graciously hand over the pot to the opener. The optimal strategy calls for a strategic retreat with these hands.

Case 2: Player A draws three cards and passes. Alas, Player A is a skeptic. He will not be bluffed out of the pot, and he dares the raiser to try to steal it. In this case Player A has only a pair and has called on far too weak a hand. To add to his problems, he gives away this damaging information in the draw. Player A has deviated from the optimal strategy; Player B can reap his just rewards from the error.

Player B should now bet all his high hands from trip Deuces or better and the corresponding number of bluff hands. But, as we shall see below, he should bet less than the pot. Trip Deuces is a strong hand now. The odds that Player A has improved his pair of Aces to trip Aces—certainly it is safe to assume that Player A would not call such a big first-round raise on any pair less than Aces—range from 1 in 7 to 1 in 13, depending on whether Player B has, or has not, seen an Ace. Thus the probability that Player A can get

Table 5.4
Player B's Second-Round Strategy After the First-Round Raise

If Player A Passes at Beginning of Second Round

Player B's Hand	Player B's Strategy		
	Player A Draws One Card	Player A Draws Two Cards	Player A Draws Three Cards
Straight or better*	Bet the pot	Bet the pot	Bet the pot
Red Queen-high four flush*	Bet the pot	Bet the pot	Bet the pot
Quads through flush†	Bet the pot	Bet the pot	Bet $\frac{3}{5}$ pot
Trip Aces through trip Queens	Bet the pot	Bet the pot	Bet $\frac{3}{5}$ pot
Trip Jacks through trip 9s	Bet the pot	Pass	Bet $\frac{3}{5}$ pot
Trip 8s through trip Deuces	Pass	Pass	Bet $\frac{3}{5}$ pot
Busted Ace-high four flush	Pass	Bet the pot	Bet $\frac{3}{5}$ pot
Busted King-high four flush	Bet the pot	Pass	Bet $\frac{3}{5}$ pot
Busted black Queen-high four flush	Pass	Pass	Pass

If Player A Bets at the Beginning of Second Round

Player A's Bet	Player B's Strategy
Bets the pot	Calls with trip 9s or better
Bets ½ pot	Calls with trip 6s or better

*The optimal strategy states that Player B should stand pat on all red Queen-high four flushes.

†On the rest of the hands in this column, Player B has drawn one card.

into the winning circle, trip Aces or better, is at most 1 in 7.

Although Player A should bet all his high hands, the bet on trips should be only three-fifths of the pot. In our example, the pot contained $90 at the beginning of the second round, and so Player B should bet only $54 on the hands to which he draws cards. His trip hands may graduate to full houses, but Player B should not publish his good fortune by varying his bet from the optimal $54. When the bet is three-fifths of the pot, the correct bluff ratio is 3:8; when Player B bets the pot, the bluff ratio is 1:2. **If Player A passes, Player B should come out with a bet of three-fifths of the pot on trip Deuces or better and on all busted Ace- and King-high four flushes. If Player B stands pat, he should come out with a second-round bet the size of the pot.**

Case 3: Player A draws two cards. Obviously, Player A does not have two pair on the first round. Is he starting off with trips or a pair—too tricky to draw three cards to his pair? If he does have only a pair, he has called with too light a hand. His chance of building the hand to trips is less than 1 in 10. But, alas, the raiser cannot ignore the possibility that Player A may very well have started with trips. That Player A passed at the beginning of the second round does not rule out his holding high trips; he could simply be cautious. Player B should definitely tighten his betting in such a situation. Trip Queens or better become the strength betting hands. This could be stretched to trip Jacks if one of the three side cards has been a Queen or better. I have seen openers with small trips trying to slow down the second-round betting with two-card draws, but Player B should still proceed with caution. See table 5.4 for precise rules.

One more tactic deserves comment. When the pot has been opened and a player with a big hand simply calls and does not raise, the tactic is called *slow playing* the hand. The object of slow playing is to appear weak and hope that some of the players yet to speak will call and, if the tactic succeeds, raise.

I strongly recommend against using first-round slow playing. When the pot has been opened and you have a big hand, *raise*. The opener has the best chance of having the biggest hand among the opposition, so hit him. Don't hope for the small miracle that a player yet to be heard from has a raising hand. If he does have a raising hand he probably will also call your raise; therefore, little is lost.

Case 4: Player A opens the pot on the first round, Player B calls and raises the pot. Player A merely calls the first-round raise. Player A draws cards but at the beginning of the second round Player A comes out with a bet the size of the pot. Player A is deviating from his optimal strategy, but that is his privilege. Player A is saying that he was not strong enough to reraise on the first round, but after the draw his hand is a whopper. But then again he could be bluffing; his miserable little two pair may not have improved, but Player A wants the pot anyway.

Player B must protect his high hand from being bluffed out. The correct strategy means calling with the top half of his strength hands—trip 9s or better. However, Player B may very well find himself facing a full house—if Player A is not bluffing, B should be very cautious about a second-round raise. The calling criterion is independent of how many cards A draws. All of the last three cases can be seen in condensed form in table 5.4.

Let us now return to a relatively rare situation mentioned earlier.

The opener reraises on the first round. The action now becomes heavy. A player looks at his hand for the second time; perhaps he has a full house, or perhaps thinks about going home and getting some sleep. In any case let us analyze the situation: The ante is $10, Player A opens for $10 in a position requiring only Jacks or better for a profitable opening, Player B calls the $10 opening bet and raises $30. (At this juncture the pot contains $60.) No other players call. Now the opener calls the $30 raise and reraises $90.

When should the first raiser, Player B, call? The principle for calling is the same for B as it was for the opener contemplating when to call B's raise. The opener, Player A, is betting $120 (the $30 call plus the $90 reraise). Player A is betting $120 to win $60. Player B should call the pot one-third of the time, that is, with the top one-third of his hands. Table 5.3 shows that Player B should raise the pot with trip 9s or better. Player B should not call a reraise that is the size of the pot with a four flush. The odds against making the flush combined with the opener's threat of holding a very strong hand are too much for a four flush. If the reraise had been smaller, anything up to $50, the four flush has reasonable odds. In a limit game B calls with a four flush.

We are concerned here with the correct strategy for Player B, but the minimal strength hand for Player A's reraising can also be computed. Player B calls the raise with the top one-third of his calling hands; the top two-fifths of B's calling hands corresponds to a straight or better. Thus Player A should have at least a straight or better—the top two-fifths of B's hands—to reraise on the first round. That Player A should make a bluff reraise goes without saying. This rule also fits in with the fact that Player A cannot hide the strength of a pat hand in the draw.

If Player B calls A's reraise with high trips, the optimal play is when Player A stands pat in the draw. This is the correct strategy for the opener, but I've seen it violated by the opener more often than obeyed. **Player A stands pat; Player B should draw two cards to his high trips, and stand pat with a straight or better; no false carding.**

There is no point in drawing one card to trips now. Player B has called the reraise, a foolish play with anything less than trips, and now Player B is desperately trying for his full house. (Drawing one card to trips, the chance of making a full house or quads is about 85 times in 1,000. Drawing two cards, the chances rise to about 105 times in 1,000. Also, if the hand improves, the chance for quads is 2 times in 5. Therefore, Player B should not be at all bashful about drawing to his hand once Player A stands pat.

Since most poker players do not follow the optimal strategy, the usual suboptimal case must also be considered.

Player A draws two cards. Player A has raised with too light a hand. Few players can resist the temptation of reraising with high trips; some philanthropists even think a reraise on low trips is a sound play.

Player B has the opportunity for a coup. Once Player A draws cards, Player B should automatically stand pat on trip 9s or 10s. Player B will make a pat bluff with these hands on the second round if Player A passes. On trips from Jacks through Aces Player B should draw two cards. When B stands pat, Player A will not know if he is bluffing;

B has effectively randomized the information in the draw. It may seem wasteful to sacrifice a good hand such as three 10s to false carding, especially when A draws two cards, but B cannot know until after he has called whether A has a pat hand. By then it is too late for B to drag in a scruffier hand, say a four flush, for false carding.

At the poker table it is important to show no hesitation when you tell the dealer that you need no cards. Any hesitation might give away your bluff. I recall one incident where in B's position I had false carded on trip 10s after A had drawn two cards. Player A passed, I bet the size of the pot, and A called the bet with the speed of light. I congratulated A on catching my bluff with such ease. He modestly rejected my praise, pointing out how much more profitable it was to play poker intuitively than scientifically. He then lay down his hand—three 8s!

If A draws cards and B stands pat, B should use the betting strategy given in table 5.4. B ignores the fact that A has reraised the pot, betting as if A had not reraised and using trip 9s and 10s for bluff hands.

Player A and Player B both stand pat. This is such a rare occurrence there is little reason to give a set of rules for further betting. The next high-hand bet should be made with a full house; about one-fifth of the pat hands are full houses.

At pot-limit poker I would not recommend that Player B re-reraise on the first round. The correct strength hand for this improbable situation is a pat full house. Even in the very unlikely game where Player B has quads and has been reraised—a once in a lifetime situation if the game is honest —I would suggest a tactical call and a wait for the second-round betting.

At this point in the game, because so much money has

already been bet, at least one of the players is running low on chips, and any further action may depend upon this consideration. (See the "all-in" rule in chapter 7.)

A FIRST-ROUND RAISE WITH THREE PLAYERS INVOLVED

There are several situations in which first-round raises involve more than two players. These plays can be covered by our previous analysis: Player A opens, Player B calls, Player C calls the opening bet and raises.

For the raiser this situation can be played almost as if Player B did not call. What are the differences? Player A still has at least an opening hand and this situation has already been analyzed. Player B may have a big hand but he only called—he did not raise—the opener. B's most profitable strategy is to raise the opener with trips or better, and only on rare occasions will his varying from the optimal strategy pay off. However, Player C should not give this unlikely variation much thought.

Player C, the raiser, should assume that Player B has at most two pair. There are several advantages for Player C. First, it only costs Player C $50 to win $30, a higher percentage return than Player B raising—risking $40 to win $20. Second, a bluff raise is more likely to succeed: Player A will certainly hesitate to call the raise with a medium sized two pair for fear that Player B will overcall with a higher two pair. Even if Player C is bluffing, Player B will reap the rewards. Also, Player B will be reluctant to call with two medium-sized pair, knowing that his previous call of the opener, not a raise, puts an upper limit on his hand. Player C should use the first-round raising strategy that was given for Player B in table 5.3. A bluff raise in this case has an excellent chance of winning the pot. Players A and B will usually fall over themselves exiting from the pot.

There is another variation of a first-round raise involving three players: The ante is $10 in a Jacks-or-better game. Player A opens for $10; Player B calls the opening bet and raises $30. Player C calls the opening bet plus the raise for $40. Player C, who could easily have remained an innocent bystander, has voluntarily decided to get in the middle of a donneybrook. Player Bs raise spelled trouble, and Player A still has a first-round chance for a reraise. The reraise possibility is small, admittedly, but should not be ignored by Player C. **Player C should not call a raised pot with any hand less than trip 6s. With a pat hand Player C should reraise.** Player C should make no attempt to conceal his hand in the draw; this is one of the rare times a player should draw two cards to his trips.

Once Player C has entered the pot, the opener's philosophy is quite different from that of facing a raise. Left alone against the raiser, Player A is strongly motivated by the possibility of a bluff raise. But once Player C has "jumped the fence," that is, called the raise when not previously involved in the pot, Player A may now be certain that at least Player C has a big hand, let alone the raiser, Player B. Player A's only concern is whether his hand is high enough for a profitable call against the big hands that are already out. **Player A has a profitable call of the raise with trip 8s or better.**

In the draw Player A should draw two cards to his trips. The promised land is now a full house or better, therefore A shouldn't lessen his chances of getting there.

First-Round Raises at a Limit Game

The difference between a limit game and a pot-limit game is most dramatically seen in the first-round raise. The basic principles are the same but the two types of games are quite different in their application. For example, the ratio (and absolute number) of bluff raises decreases drastically in a low-limit game. So in the play it appears that first-round bluff raises do not exist. The appearance is illusory, however, for first-round bluff raises do exist, albeit much less frequently. Another difference is that the opener should definitely call a raise on one-pair hands and draw three cards. This play is usually limited to a pair of Aces.

Let us examine different types of limit games and derive the optimal strategies for each.

Example 1: The game is $10–$20 limit Jacks-or-better draw poker. All first-round bets are limited to $10, and all second-round bets are limited to $20. The ante is $10 and Player A has opened the pot for $10. (For purposes of simplification, assume that Player A has opened in any position where a pair of Jacks is a profitable opening hand.) Player B calls the $10 opening bet and raises $10. On what hands should Player B raise and on what hands should Player A call?

The last question first. Player B is betting $20 to win $20, the $10 ante plus Player A's opening bet. Player A should call the $10 raise with the top 50 percent of his opening hands.

To translate this idea into hands is not as easy as before.

135

Referring to table 5.1, we see that the top half of Player A's opening hands may be as low as a pair of Aces. In a limit game it is better to call with a pair of Aces than with two small pair.

Player A should call with two pair, 8s and 5s or better, a pair of Aces or Kings, with an Ace kicker, (for example, K, K, A, x, y).

The raising hand for Player B should consist of the usual two parts: the strength hands and the bluff-raising hands, but because of the low limit, the bluff raising hands are severely limited.

Player B should raise with trip Deuces or better or Ace-high four flushes (with the exception of A-K-high or A-Q-high four flushes, on which he should call).

Suppose Player A calls the first-round raise, draws cards, and does the proper thing of passing to Player B on the second round?

Player B then draws one card to all hands, except when he stands pat with true pat hands—straights or better—or Ace-Jack-high four flushes.

Player B comes out with a bet on the second round, $20, on all hands to which he drew one card: trip 5s or better or all busted four flushes.

Player B bets all hands when he stood pat. Player A should then call with the top five-sevenths of his hands and raise on trip Queens or better, with the appropriate number of bluff hands.

Example 2: The game, again Jacks-or-better draw poker, has a $10 ante and a $50 limit on all bets.

This is so close to a pot-limit game we need not spell out different rules. Use the strategies for Player A and B given in tables 5.2 and 5.3. The main exception is that Player B

136

should not make quite as many bluff raises, not raise on black Queen-high four flushes. The $50 limit cuts down on the optimal number of bluff raises needed for his second-round betting.

Example 3: The game is Chicago pot limit in which a player can bet the pot, computed before he has put any money into it. For example, if the ante is $10 Player A can open the pot for $10, but when the pot comes to Player B he can either call the $10 bet or call and raise $10. The pot was only $20 when it came time for Player B to act. This version is far closer to Example 1, although the second round would allow bets of $50, meaning Player B should use slightly more bluff hands. This version puts a severe restriction on first-round bluff raises.

Example 4: The game is table stakes. Assume that both Player A and B have several hundred dollars in chips. Assume the ante is $10 and Player A opens for $10. Player B would like to raise. He can legally raise more than $30, but the simplest rule for him is to raise only the pot, and this was covered earlier in the chapter.

Summary

Player A opens the pot on the first round, Player B calls the opening bet and raises the size of the pot.

Player A's strategy. If A opens with a pair of Jacks or Queens, he is essentially out to steal the ante. If he is called on the first round he has poor prospects of holding the best hand unless he is fortunate in the draw. Even a pair of Kings doesn't give him much chance against a first-round caller, not, that is, if the caller knows how to play the game. With a pair of Aces or two small pair A's prospects improve, but a lonely pair of Aces only serves as a bluff catcher against a second-round bet. But in this case A is faced with a first-round raise.

Even with a medium sized two-pair, A's chances still do not look too promising. But Player A's problem is that if he does not call in the two-pair range he will be bluffed out of far too many pots. The raiser is laying the odds, saying he has a big hand, but he is not under oath. The raiser could have a nothing hand, attempting larceny with his raise.

Player A is forced to call the raise with two medium sized pair, and he should certainly call the raise with trips. But now he must be cautious because the raiser says that he has the muscle. Player A, therefore, meekly calls the raiser with all hands from medium sized two-pairs through trip Aces. Player A draws one card, modestly passes, and awaits the second-round deluge.

Player B's strategy. A good percentage of the time Player B's raise will be a bluff raise. He will be raising the pot on a hand that does not even qualify for calling. But when B is not bluffing he should have a very strong hand. The smallest strong hand that dictates a raise is trip Deuces. However, even with trip Deuces, B must not venture a raise if the opener needed a hand bigger than a pair of Jacks for a profitable opening hand; calling would then be in order.

Player B must not show his heroics by raising with two pair. This is probably the worst play in poker, it is also one of the most frequent errors. Two-pair hands are reasonable first-round calling hands, but it would be foolish to take short odds on them. And this is exactly what a player would be doing by making a first-round raise.

If you are in a game where the opener guarantees a call on all raises, then certainly two pair gives enough odds, but only when the opener is so stubborn that he never folds when faced with a raise. If you know such players, then raise with two pair; in fact a pair of Aces would then give you sufficient odds. But the opener is usually not forced to call all raises and in almost any game worth playing, the opener will not call with a lonely pair.

Of course you will have no guarantee that the opener will even call with two pair; he might wait for trip 10s or better. For this reason you must have the correct mixture of bluff hands that give you the maximum guaranteed profit over all of your raising hands (optimal strategy). These bluff-raise hands will consist of selected four flushes.

The optimal second-round betting strategy must incorporate any information that comes your way in the draw. The opener who calls the raise and draws three cards says he is weak and Player B should use that information to clobber him. The opener who draws one card, and especially two cards, must be treated with caution. Some of your small trip hands should not be too eager to engage in any further betting; if the opener passes, with these hands you will also gladly pass and see who wins in the showdown.

It is interesting now to apply our theory and rules to particular problems. As in chapter 4, we ask the reader to be one of the players; we give the hand and all the relevant information, who bet what and when, and the number of cards drawn by each player. Applications by means of problems always help in understanding a theoretical approach.

Problems

Problem 1: In a seven-handed, Jacks-or-better, pot-limit game with a $10 ante, you are Player B. Your hand on the first round is QH, 7H, 6H, 3H, AC.

Player	A	B
Position	4	6
First Round	Opens for $10	Calls the $10 and raise $30
	Calls the $30 raise	
Draw	Two cards	?

How many cards should you, Player B, draw? Against a one-card draw you should stand pat if playing the optimal strategy. Should you alter your plans if Player A is not playing optimally, that is, if he is drawing two cards?

Answer: The fact that Player A is drawing two cards should in no way deter you from going ahead with your pat bluff. The only thing that might alter your plan is if Player A stands pat. A one card draw would then be in order.

The red Queen-high four flushes were chosen in planning the optimal strategy because it gives the correct number of hands for the optimal bluff ratio and because this criterion

140

is easy to remember. Just think of the Red Queen in *Alice In Wonderland.* You should stand pat.

Problem 2: In a seven-handed, Jacks-or-better, pot-limit game with a $10 ante, you are Player C. Your hand on the first round is AH, KD, QH, JD, 10S; on the second round, AH, KD, QH, JD, 10S.

Player	A	B	C
Position	3	5	6
First Round	Opens for $10	Calls the opening $10	Calls the opening bet and raises $30
	Calls the raise	Folds	
Draw	No cards		No cards
Second Round	Pass		?

How do you, Player C, plan the second round?

Answer: The answer involves more questions. What information have you revealed about your hand? Certainly you have given every indication of at least a straight. If you bluff raised on the first round with a red Queen-high four flush (see table 5.3), planning to stand pat, you certainly should have altered your plans after Player A stood pat. Then you should have drawn one card for a free shot at your flush.

What information do you have about Player A's hand? There are three possibilities. First, Player A may have a small straight and is just too cautious to make a first-round reraise. Second, he may be trying some irregular play with a hand such as two pair, planning to make a second-round bluff if you draw cards. Third, Player A may have a power-house, say a high full house. His first-round failure to reraise may have been intended to lure Player B in over his head.

141

In the first and second possibilities, a second-round bet would gain nothing. Player A would fold. In the third case, a bet would bring on the deluge.

You should pass, turn over your hand, and watch the action from the sidelines.

Problem 3: In a seven-handed, Jacks-or-better, pot-limit game with a $10 ante, you are Player A. Your hand on the first round is 7H, 7C, 7S, 5C, 2C; on the second round, 7H, 7C, 7S, 2C, 5D.

Player	A	B
Position	5	7
First Round	Opens for $10	Calls $10 and raises $30
	Calls the $30 raise	
Draw	One card	Three cards
Second Round	?	

How should you, Player A, play the second round, especially after Player B raised and then drew three cards?

Answer: Player B has made a foolish first-round raise and then blandly admitted it by drawing three cards. Use Muggins Law. You should treat B like the simpleton that he is: Pass to him. Player B is clearly in the pot with too light a hand.

You should pass at the beginning of the second round and be willing to call any bet by Player B. Another example of dealing with a Muggins.

Problem 4: In a six-handed, Jacks-or-better, pot-limit game with a $10 ante, you are Player A. Your hand on the first round is KS, KC, 7H, 2D, 4H.

Player	A	B
Position	5	4
First Round	—	Pass
	$10 open	$10 call and a $30 raise
	?	

What action should you, Player A, take after being raised by Player B, a player who passed in position 4 in a six-handed game?

Answer: This problem takes up a topic left unanswered in chapter 5, that is, how to deal with a raiser in a very late position who raises after passing. Certainly Player B's action is *verboten* according to the optimal strategy. Nevertheless, you will certainly encounter this aberration at the table. Player B's action seems to say that he is bluffing. He could not even open and yet here he is raising. The opener should treat every raise in much the same way, namely call with the top one-third of his opening hands. In this case a pair of Kings is too light a hand to take on a raise. You should fold.

There is a possibility that you have given away the fact that you were going to open by prematurely touching your chips, a facial gesture, or some comment. Possibly Player B might even have had a peek at your cards before he acted. In any case, you should give his tactics some thought. A cautious player often will not even look at his hand before it is his turn to act, a tactic that I recommend in a tough game. It is impossible to tip off a hand that you have not seen.

Problem 5: In a seven-handed, Jacks-or-better, pot-limit game with a $10 ante, you are Player D. Your hand on the first round is JS, JH, JD, JC, 4S.

Player	A	B	C	D
Position	2	4	6	1
First Round	—	—	—	Pass
	$10 open	$10 call	$10 call and a $40 raise	?

How should you, Player D, play the first round?

Answer: You have a hand that is as close to a sure thing as you can have at high-draw poker. Your only concern is to maximize the pot. Your hand also has cover in the draw. Namely, you can draw one card without revealing the strength of your hand. The best way to maximize the pot in this case is to slowplay the hand. Play possum: Only call the raise.

There are two reasons for this. First, Player A might call or even reraise if the stars are right. He opened in Position 2, indicating an above average hand. Player B's position also indicates strength. Second, Player C might be bluffing, so a reraise now might win the pot outright with no further profits. So give Player C a chance to keep bluffing or possibly make his flush.

CHAPTER 6

Second-Round Strategy for Three or More Players

Facing several opponents in a big pot is one of the reasons poker is the most interesting of all card games. When there have been no first-round raises—the situation we are considering here—the only player with first-round power is the opener. The opener is the only player that need concern himself with false carding in the draw, and the only player that might have enough strength for a second-round bet no matter how he fares in the draw. The opener may or may not have a full house but he should certainly make his opponents pay to find out.

The strategies given in chapters 3 and 4 applied to openers facing only one opponent in the second round. A good player must master these bread-and-butter plays. Against more than one opponent the tactics become more complicated; but because the rewards increase as well, it is worth the effort to master these more sophisticated plays.

Opener's Strategy: The Squeeze and the Option-Squeeze Play

In analyzing a round in which more than two players are in action we must carefully describe all the circumstances. Who is in what seat and how many cards each player draws now become critical pieces of information.

In planning the optimal strategy, we've discussed two distinct cases. In the first case the opener is called by a player who had originally passed. In this situation the caller backs into the pot, is not in Position 1 or 2, and draws one card. This player is called an *inactive caller*. In this case the opener can profitably assume that the caller holds a four flush. The opener's strategy, then, is to draw down to his hand and pass. The only strategic consideration is how often to call a second-round bet by the caller and this we have discussed thoroughly in chapter 3.

In the second case the opener has one caller, whose calling hand is a mystery. The caller did not pass on the first round. If the caller draws three cards, the mystery is dispelled; but if the caller draws one card, the opener cannot know whether the caller is drawing to two pair or to a four flush. We discussed the strategy for this situation in chapter 4: The opener must be willing to make a second-round bet without complete information.

148

When facing two callers on the second round the situation is even more complex. The opener has two uncertainties to face. Can he decide anything about the types of hands either of the two callers has?

The easiest situation to deal with is when the opener is faced with two four-flush callers, both of whom are inactive callers. If both callers passed on the first round but then backed in once the pot was opened, and both callers draw one card, the opener probably has two four flushes after him. The opener had better draw down to his hand and pass at the beginning of the second round. His only decision is how often to call a bet by Player B or by Player C. This situation, an extension of chapter 3, is analyzed in the last part of this chapter.

The more common situation, however, is when the opener has no information about the first caller. Player B calls the first-round bet without having originally passed. With respect to Player C, the second caller, the opener may or may not have any information. Player C may have backed into the pot and drawn one card. However, the opener must effectively plan a strategy without a clear picture of what Player B is drawing to; he must false card before knowing Player B's draw.

For example: It is a seven-handed game, the ante is $10, and Player A in Position 5 opens for $10. Player B in Position 6 calls for $10 and finally Player C in Position 4 calls, backing in, for $10. In the draw Player C draws one card.

Players A and B are now under the shadow of Player C, since Player C will probably have the best hand if he makes his four flush. As mentioned, the correct method of minimizing the winnings of the four flusher is for the opener to pass. When the opener faces only one opponent drawing to a four

149

flush, he automatically passes on the second round, waiting to see if the four flusher bets. If in the three-person case Player A passes, then for Player B's own safety Player B should also pass.

Thus, Player A should pass to minimize the winnings of Player C, but will this maximize the winnings of Player A? When only two people are in the pot, to minimize your opponent's winnings will, of course, maximize your own winnings. But when three people are in the pot, to minimize the winnings of one opponent will not necessarily maximize your own. You might just be sweetening the pot for the third player. Every player must look out for himself in poker. If you can profitably put one of your opponents in a cement mixer, this antisocial behavior is what the game is all about.

Let us return to the specific situation. Suppose that Player A automatically passes on the second round. Player B should then pass, for his own safety, and Player C should come out with a bet the size of the pot when he has made his flush and bluff using the 1:2 bluff ratio.

What now happens to Player A? If Player C is using the correct 1:2 bluff ratio (one bluff hand for every two flushes), then on the average Player A cannot make any money by calling with anything less than a full house. If Player A has trip 10s and he calls Player C, one out of three times he will beat Player C. But if Player A catches Player C bluffing, there is a possibility that Player B will overcall with higher trips. Thus Player A has a chance of losing even if Player C is bluffing.

If Player C passes, then all the players will turn over their hands, and Player A's trip 10s have a good chance to win a relatively small pot.

Now trace the play when, at the beginning of the second

round, Player A decides to bet. This puts Player B in the wringer. Even if Player A is bluffing and Player B calls with two pair or trips, Player C will overcall or raise when he has made his flush. However, if Player B does not start calling, Player C is unable to call a bet unless he has made his flush. Thus, if Player A can bluff Player B, he has about a four-out-of-five chance of winning the pot. (Player C makes his flush only about 9 times in 47.)

Player A's best strategy is to use the threat of Player C's overcalling to intimidate Player B. Because Player C cannot call unless he makes his flush, Player A's strategy is to bluff Player B out of the pot much more frequently than if Player C were not there.

In most poker games, Player A and B will automatically pass to the four flush, in a sense forming a coalition to limit the profits of Player C. However, Player A is subsidizing this coalition.

THE SQUEEZE

If Player A comes out with a bet, the coalition is now between Players A and C. Certainly Player C is quite happy with the prospect of having Player A bet, especially when Player C has made his flush. By betting, Player A raises his own potential profits. Player A will raise the winnings of Player C by betting and will throw Player B into a state of economic depression. But most important, Player A earns a greater profit than by automatically passing. This pressure play by Player A is called a *squeeze play;* the squeeze is on Player B. The elements of the squeeze strategy are how much to bet, on what strength hands, and how frequently to bluff.

Player A cannot bet too loosely—after all, Player A does

not want to martyr himself on Player C's flushes. Furthermore, Player A must tie his strategy to the probability that he has a full house. For this reason Player A should draw one card to trips, two pair, and a certain number of bluff hands. (There is a detailed discussion of an analogous situation for the opener in chapter 4.) The bluff hands will consist of a certain percentage of a lonely pair of Jacks or Queens.

Because of Player C's presence, the bluff ratio is higher than in the two-person situation. For example, if C were not present, Player A's bet of one-third the pot would call for a bluff ratio of 1:4; but with Player C backing in, A's bluff ratio rises to 1:3.

The squeeze play is valid whether a player draws one, three, or no cards. The amount of his bet should vary with the number of cards he draws. (See table 6.1 for all the details.) Again the best bet is not the size of the pot, but varies from one-third to one-half the pot.

The squeeze play works best when A stands pat, but how often is a player dealt a pat hand? Furthermore, Player A will only try a squeeze play after drawing three cards when Player B also has drawn three cards (see table 6.2). Actually, if the reader understands the strategy of chapter 4 he will have a good feel for the squeeze play.

SQUEEZE-OPTION PLAY

A squeeze-option play is the opener's optimal strategy against two callers when the second caller did not back into the pot. This is a common situation when the opener is in an early position at the table. The opener must plan to false card with no knowledge of the number of cards that each of the callers is drawing.

Table 6.1

Squeeze Play: The Opener's Strategy Against Two Callers—
Player B Does Not Back into the Pot on the First Round; Player
C Has Backed into the Pot and Has Drawn One Card

First-Round Hand	Number of Cards Drawn	Second-Round Hand	Percentage of Pot Bet
True pat hand, straight or better	None	Straight or better	One-half
A pair of Jacks or Queens*	None	One pair	One-half
Trips or quads	One	Full house	One-third
Two pair	One	Trips	One-third
		Two pairs	Pass
Pair of Jacks or Queens†	One	An unimproved pair	One-third

*When both Jacks or Queens are of the same color and all side cards are of the same color.
†A pair of Jacks when all the side cards are 9 or less; a pair of Queens when all the side cards are 7 or less.

If both Players B and C draw three cards, then Player A has important information, and any trip hand or better is worth a bet. But the chances of either Player B or C coming up with high trips is around 1 in 4, indicating that only a moderate bet is appropriate. The correct bet is one-half the pot.

If Player C draws one card, then Player C could either have two pair or a four flush on the first round. In practice, few players can resist coming in as the second caller with a four straight, although this is not sound play. When Player C draws one card it increases his chances of beating trips and lowers his chances of having a hand that could beat a pair of Jacks. Thus, Player A should bet less and bluff more than the size of the bet would indicate.

Table 6.2

Squeeze Play: The Opener's Strategy Against Two Callers—
Player B Has Drawn Three Cards; Player C Has Backed into the
Pot and Drawn One Card

First-Round Hand	Number of Cards Drawn	Second-Round Hand	Percentage of Pot Bet
All pairs that didn't qualify for the one card or pat squeeze	Three	Full house	One-fourth
		Trip Aces	One-fourth
		Trips*	One-fourth
		A pair of Jacks or Queens†	One-fourth
		All other hands	Pass

*All trip Kings, Queens, or Jacks, having seen one Ace.
†All pairs of Jacks and Queens, having seen two Aces.

On the squeeze-option play, Player A draws one card to trips, two pair, and a pair of Jacks (when all the side cards are 9 or less). On all trips or better and on the unimproved pair of Jacks, Player A comes out with a second-round bet depending upon the number of cards that Player C draws. The option comes in selecting the size of the bet at the last moment. If Player C draws three cards, Player A bets one-half the pot. (See table 6.3). If Player C draws one card, then Player A bets one-third the pot.

The same type of play occurs when the opener stands pat, but because of the strength of high hands the bets are larger.

Opener versus Two Four Flushes

There is one final strategy for the second round: The opener is faced with two callers both of whom have backed in the pot on the first round and have drawn one card. The correct conclusion for the opener is that both callers are drawing to four flushes. When the opener is faced with two four flushes, his strategy is very similar to having only one four flush to contend with. The draw and the beginning of the second-round betting is exactly the same.

Player A, the opener, draws down to all of his hands,

Table 6.3
Squeeze-Option Play: The Opener's Strategy Against
Two Callers—Neither Caller Has Backed into the Pot

First-Round Hand, Player Draws One Card to	Second-Round Hand	Percentage of Pot Bet
Trips or Quads	Quads through Trip Deuces†	One-half if C draws three cards, one-third if C draws one card.
Two Pair	All two pair	Pass
Pair Jacks*	Unimproved pair of Jacks	One-half if C draws three cards, one-third if C draws one card.

*A pair of Jacks when all the side cards are 9 or less.

†The top 24 percent of these high-betting hands are at least a full house. If any player raises the size of the pot, Player A calls with trip Jacks or better.

155

except a pair of Aces with a King kicker. On these hands the opener stands pat—the poverty bluff. Player A automatically passes at the beginning of the second round.

The problem that Player A faces is how frequently to call a bet by either Player B or Player C. If Player B bets, Player A has one thing working for him; namely, if Player C makes his flush, Player C would call a bet by Player B.

Player C helps solve Player A's calling problem when Player C makes his flush, and Player C will make his flush one-fifth of the time. Once Player C either calls or raises a bet by Player B, Player A should not even think of calling with anything less than a very high flush. In the remaining four-fifths of the time, how frequently should Player A call a bet by Player B? Player A must make certain that Player B is not going to make money by his bluffs and, as we have seen in chapter 3, Player A must see that Player B is called a certain percentage of the time.

Let us examine the problem in the following manner: Suppose that Player B bets the size of the pot ten times. The maximal strategy for Player A is to make certain that Player B is called one-half of the time. Now Player C will make his flush two times out of ten, and he will call Player B. Out of the remaining eight times when Player C does not make his flush and cannot call, Player A should call Player B three times, that is, Player A should call Player B three-eighths of the time when Player C does not call.

We have now arrived at the first rule for Player A: **If Player B bets and Player C folds, Player A should call with the top three-eighths of his hands.**

The only remaining problem for Player A is when Player B passes and Player C bets. Player A should regard this situation as if Player B were not in the game; he should use the same strategy he used against only one four flush. We can show that if Player B makes his flush and sandbags, that is, passes at the beginning of the second round, Player B will merely limit his winnings and increase Player A's winnings. **If Player B passes and Player C bets the size of the pot, Player A should call with the top one-half of his hands.**

See table 3.1 for the distribution of the opener's hand after the draw.

PLAYER B'S SECOND-ROUND STRATEGY AGAINST
TWO OR MORE OPPONENTS

Player B is in a difficult situation against two opponents. He deserves more than our sympathy; let us give him some help with his strategy in the following examples.

Example 1: The ante is $10; the action is:

Player	A	B	C
Position	4	6	1
First Round	—	—	Pass
	Open $10	$10 call	$10 call
Draw	Pat	Three cards	Three cards
Second Round	$40 bet	?	

The pot contains $40 at the end of the first round, and Player A, after standing pat, comes roaring out with a $40 bet. Player B looks down at his hand and sees that he has caught another King giving him trip Kings. What should Player B do? Call, fold, or start screaming?

The answer is fold. Even if Player A is bluffing, the threat of Player C's overcalling with trip Aces (and a good player in C's position would not overcall with anything less than trip Aces) will make bluff catching a losing proposition. If C were not present, a call by Player B would be in order, since

157

trip Kings would be the bluff catcher. But with C as an active caller behind, leave the bluff catching to Player C.

The implication is not that Player B should never call with trip Kings, but rather that he should call only if the hand has some prospect of beating some of A's high-betting hands. In our example, if Player A had drawn cards, then Player B should certainly call with trip Kings.

Example 2: The ante is $10, the action has been:

Player	A	B	C
Position	5	6	3
First Round	—	—	Pass
	$10 open	$10 call	$10 call
Draw	One card	Three cards	One card
Second Round	$20 bet	?	

At the end of the first round the pot contained $40, and Player A has come out with a bet of $20 at the beginning of the second round. Player B has caught another pair, giving him Kings-up on the second round. Should Player B call?

This is precisely the situation for the squeeze play, and Player B is caught with a medium-sized hand. However, Player B must bite the bullet and call. (Incidentally, if Player A were a weak player, not realizing the technical subtleties of the squeeze play, if I were Player B, I would probably fold. But against a good player or a player who has read this book, I would call.)

Because of the squeeze play, in the first round a player must be very cautious about calling. Many pros will not make a first-round call with anything less than a pair of Aces, although this is unnecessarily conservative.

If Player A passes, Player B can relax, his prospects of winning improve, and he is not subject to all manner of traps.

158

With only one exception, Player B should also pass. The exception is when Player C draws three cards and Player B draws only one card. (Player A's draw is irrelevant, only Player A's pass is relevant.) We are not in the squeeze situation as Player C drew three cards. Now Player B bets the size of the pot, using the strategy from chapter 4, see table 4.5.

If there is more than one caller behind Player B, he should always pass.

Summary

This chapter was an extension of the optimal strategy, whose basic principles were developed in chapter 4 and then applied to the second most common situation in draw poker—the three-man second round. Two new ideas were introduced. First, if a player is bluffing, it is no more painful to be called twice rather than once. Second, although an inactive caller drawing one card—a four flusher—has potentially high, even raising, hands he does not have middle-class bluff-catching hands. These two ideas were behind the different types of squeeze plays, and a good player should master Player A's different techniques in a three-man second round. For the four-handed second round, all the opener need remember is to pass.

In our examples, the pot at the end of the first round contained $40. Player A should use his bets with the dexterity of a fencer; he cannot afford to be a barbarian hoisting a battle axe. Smaller and more frequent bets—the thrusts and parries of poker—are more profitable in this situation than the bludgeon of the big bet. A bet of one-third to one-half the pot is usually more appropriate than a pot-sized bet. These techniques are not unknown to good players in a limit game, but in a table-stakes or pot-limit game the subtlety is often lost.

In the analysis of the squeeze play I mentioned a "coalition." I did not mean to imply an illegal alliance formed before the game. Nor do I mean the often unconscious union formed by two old friends. Rather, the coalition is a natural pooling of interests based on each individual's position and draw. These legal coalitions form, realign, and then splinter into a fight for the spoils. The squeeze play is merely a coalition between Players A and C at the start of second-round betting, rather than the traditional coalition between A and B. It is often an amusing and profitable pastime to analyze (silently) other players' actions in terms of these fleeting and fluctuating coalitions.

CHAPTER 7

Poker Variations and Advanced Problems

I hope that this book has given you a reliable strategy for playing draw poker. I also hope that I have made clear the basis for analyzing a wide variety of games, for if I have, you are in a position to analyze for yourself the many variations of poker.

At the end of this chapter you will find a set of rather difficult problems. These situations have appeared, and will do so again, many times at the poker table. I cannot guarantee that your opponents will play their optimal strategy, so the question arises of who is being lured into whose trap. This is where style, tact, and finesse come into the game.

Although the classic versions of poker are endlessly fascinating, modern man has altered the rules, changed the deck, and even tampered with the very soul of poker to create a richer variety for his jaded palate. Merely to list all the variations would take another book, and to list the various strategies would require an encyclopedia. This is why I have limited the discussion to high-draw poker. You will find nary a mention of such civilized games as low draw, the many variations of stud, the innumerable variations of hi-lo poker, hold-em, and on and on. I confess that I find some of these heresies fascinating, but space does not permit any more analysis or strategy.

If you are an active poker player, eventually you will be invited to join a game that includes some of the more bizarre variants of poker. Various methods are used to jazz up poker. First, wild cards may be added to the game, and second, new types of high hands can be defined.

Deuces Wild

The classic example of adding *wild cards* is the game of Deuces wild. Wild cards are designated at the beginning of the game as cards that may be given any value, according to the needs of the hand. Deuces wild is played with the usual rules for draw poker, except that a player can let a Deuce stand for any card he pleases. For example: The hand JJ227 is redefined to be a hand containing four Jacks—each Deuce stands for a Jack. The addition of wild cards vastly inflates high hands, and betting standards must be raised accordingly. The game then becomes the usual draw game with a reevaluation of the high hands.

It is hard to understand the interest in playing Deuces wild over plain draw without wild cards. Let me give some of the reasons. There is a serious drawback to the game: A hand containing two Deuces is probably a fairly good hand, because your holding the two Deuces greatly lowers the chances that any opponent has more than one Deuce. The simple rule of play is: **Only start betting or calling when you have at least two or more wild cards** (which happens frequently enough) **or when you have a large hand such as three Kings with one wild card.**

Certain oddities can occur in this game. Suppose on the second round you have four 6s with a 4 as a side card. This is a powerful hand in regular draw poker. However, your hand contains no wild cards. This depreciates it for Deuces wild. If the betting gets heavy on the second round, it may very well not pay to call because there is a good chance of running into a larger four of a kind. But suppose the next time you have the hand 6, 6, 2, 2, 4—again four 6s with a 4 as a side card. Your hand is the same value as before, but having two wild cards makes your hand far stronger. The chances of your being beaten out now are far less. The value of a hand is both how high the hand is and how many wild cards it contains.

By playing a cautious strategy and properly evaluating your hand, you should be reasonably successful; but the game will soon degenerate into a game where the player with the most Deuces usually wins. This game is certainly a dull affair.

Using the Bug

One interesting variation, milder than introducing wild cards, adds some zest to draw poker. A 53-card deck is used, a standard poker deck with the addition of a card called the Bug. The Bug looks like a Joker, a jester picking his nose, and can be used for an Ace or a card that completes a straight or flush.

Example: The hand Bug, 2S, 3H, 4C, 6D would be a six-high straight, the bug standing for a 5. Similarly Bug, KH, 8H, 7H, 4H would be a flush, here the Bug would stand for the Ace of hearts, and so the flush would be an Ace-King-high flush.

Playing draw with a Bug has three advantages and one serious disadvantage. First, the deck introduces delightful gambling hands, such as 16- and 12-way four straights. The hand Bug, 3H, 4S, 5H, 9D on the first round would be a 16-way four straight. By discarding the 9D and drawing one card, there are 16 cards that will give you a straight: an Ace, Deuce, six, or seven. Similarly, the hand Bug, 3H, 4H, 6S, 10D would be a 12-way straight; a worthless hand or a very high hand depending on the draw.

Second, the chances of making a flush increase from 9/47 (.19) with a regular deck to 10/48 (.21) with a Bug deck.

Third, there are the marvelous "eat your cake and have it too" hands such as Bug, Ace S, KS, 5S, 10D on the first round. By discarding the 10D, the probability of a flush are .21, trip Aces or better .27, and the chances of at least Aces-up are .40. Even if the hand does not improve, it is still a solid pair of Aces, King-high.

The disadvantage is that the Bug introduces five Aces into

the deck, and thus seriously devalues the one-pair hands other than Aces, and two-pair hands other than Aces-up. Now the requirements for the first caller rise to a pair of Aces, making the game a bit tighter and less interesting.

(I could propose a more interesting version of the game by introducing to the standard deck a "Junior Bug." The Junior Bug would stand either for a Jack or a card completing a straight or flush.)

The strategy for playing draw with a Bug is similar to the regular strategy with two main exceptions. A slightly tighter opening rule is demanded, and more caution is needed to be the first caller with a pair of Kings. There is no need to elaborate additional refinements; the two games are not that different.

The distribution of opening hands given in table 7.1 is about the same as the distribution of opening hands without the Bug. However, there are a few startling differences, differences that might affect your betting.

The number of pat straights in a regular deck is about 10,200; this number increases to 20,700 when the Bug is used. So the number of possible straights increases by over 100 percent. The number of pat flushes and full houses increases from about 9,100 to 12,400 when the Bug is used, an increase of 40 percent. The probability that a pat hand is a flush or better is 47 percent when playing with a regular deck, but this decreases to 40 percent when using the Bug.

Suppose you have an Ace-high straight in a limit game. Player A opens, you call and raise, Player A reraises, and you call his raise. In the draw both you and Player A stand pat, and now Player A passes to you. What do you do?

The answer depends on whether you have the Bug or not. If you have the Bug, Player A has a pat hand out of a deck

POKER STRATEGY

Table 7.1

Distribution of Opening Hands When Playing With the Bug

Hand	Number of Hands	Percentage of All Opening Hands
Straight flush or better*	205	.03
Four of a kind or better	1,033	.16
Full house or better	5,401	.85
Flush or better	13,205	2.1
Straight or better	33,941	5.3
Three Aces or better	44,501	7.0
Three 10s or better	62,101	9.7
Three 6s or better	79,701	12.5
Three 2s or better	97,301	15.2
Aces-up or better	128,981	20.2
Kings-up or better	146,801	23.0
Queens-up or better	163,001	25.5
Jacks-up or better	177,581	27.8
9s-up or better	201,881	31.6
3s-up or better	235,901	37.0
Pair of Aces or better	373,805	58.5
Pair of Kings or better	463,565	68.3
Pair of Queens or better	551,325	86.3
Pair of Jacks or better	639,085	100.0

Other Hands of Interest When Using the Bug	
Hand	Number of Such Hands
16-Way Straight	14,400
12-Way straight	41,040
Four flush with Bug	110,940
Four flush with Bug and an Ace	9,504

*Four Aces and the Bug beats a straight flush.

without a Bug, and the probability that you have the best hand is very close to .50, which certainly does not give you enough of an edge to make a bet and face a possible reraise.

However, if you have an Ace-high straight without the Bug, your opponent's pat hand is out of a deck containing the Bug, and now you have around .60 probability that you are the winner. You now have a bet, provided that the limit is sufficiently small compared with the size of this raised and reraised pot.

The moral of this tale is that a straight without the Bug is stronger than the same sized straight with the Bug.

Advanced Problems

So far we have analyzed the most common situations in draw poker. We have examined the logic of the situation and given explicit rules for dealing with it. Now let us apply your knowledge to some of the pitfalls you would run into in a tough game. Some people play erratically and foolishly and the other players try to take advantage of this frailty.

I have known poker pros who play only a fair-to-middling game of poker against good players but are sharks in slicing up a weak player. I have also known super-pros who are specialists in looking weak but turn out to be deadly traps for the greedy. You must learn two important skills: how to profit from the other players' mistakes and how to avoid the other players' traps.

It is not difficult to learn how to profit from other players' mistakes. Some optimistic players will call and draw four cards, some will even take five cards in the draw, others will draw two cards to a flush. The list of other players' mistakes is endless. The most effective ways of profiting from their careless plays are gained by experience. It is more important

169

(especially when playing against good players) to avoid traps and sucker plays. A sucker play lures you into a disasterous pot or, conversely, frightens you out of a good pot. In order to play good poker, you must not be overly cautious, but you must be alert to warnings in time to avoid the sucker plays.

The "all-in" rule. Our first problem involves the "all-in" rule—a player may only bet or call the number of chips that he has before him when the hand is dealt, but he gets full action on his money. An example will best explain this rule.

Example 1: Player A and Player B are in a pot containing $60. Player A has $100 left and Player B has only $5.

If Player A bets $50, Player B, if he desires, can call the bet for $5, all he has left. Player A then takes back $45, ($50 − 5), and the player with the best hand wins the $70 pot ($60 + 5 + 5).

If we change our example so that Player B has no chips left, then the player with the best hand wins the $60 pot: an example of showdown—the best hand wins with no betting complications.

Example 2: The pot is again $60, Player A has $100, Player B has $5, and Player C $40.

Now if Player A bets $60 and Player B calls for $5, Player C calls for $40. There is a main pot $60 + 5 + 5 + 5 = $75; the player who has the best hand wins this pot. A side pot of $35 + 35 is a contest only between Players A and C, and Player A takes back $20 of his original bet. Of Player A's $60 bet, $5 went into the main pot and $35 went into the side pot. All of Player B's $5 went into the main pot, and finally $5 of C's call went into the main pot and the remaining $35 went into a side pot.

Clearly we could have many side pots with plenty of confusion if there were many players with different but small amounts of chips clamoring to get at the pot. This confusion is avoided in some games by a rule that each player must have a reasonable number of chips before each hand. The rest of this chapter is devoted to examples of traps and standard plays that you will run into in a good game. Up to this point, you have been using the strategy set forth in this book. What the other players are up to is not known; it is only known that none of them are duffers. In the problems presented below, you are given the number of players, the type of game, and the betting rules. In a pot-limit game, a player may bet or raise no more than is in the pot. In a $10 to $20 limit game, a player may bet or raise $10 on the first round and $20 on the second round. The total ante is fixed at $10 to facilitate explanations.

Your hand is given, and you are asked to plan the best strategy at a certain juncture in the play. The convention is again used that the opener on the first round is always called Player A, the next caller is Player B, and so on. Again, a player's position is the number of seats from the left of the dealer.

Problem 1: In a seven-handed, pot-limit, Jacks-or-better game with a $10 ante, you are Player C. Your hand before the draw is JS, 10S, 5S, 2S, 8H; your hand after the draw is JS, 10S, 5S, 2S, 7S.

Player	A	B	C
Position	5	7	4
First-round betting	-	-	Pass
Cards drawn	Three	Three	One
Second-round betting	Pass (forced)	Pass	?

171

After the ante Player A had only $10 left, and so after he opened Player A is all in. Both you and Player B each have over $300 in chips. How should you, Player C, bet your flush?

Answer: First, because you backed into the pot in a late position and drew one card, your hand is marked as a four flush or a four straight. Second, you cannot bluff; you must have either a straight or a flush on the second round because a bluff would not gain any money. Third, if you bluff you cannot force A out of the pot since he is all in; thus a busted four flush will make no money.

The least you could bet with is a straight. Thus, Player B would only call (and probably raise) with a full house. You are essentially playing with your cards face up.

Proper Play: Your best, optimal and maximal, strategy is to not bet, pass, turn over your flush, and start to reach for the pot.

I have assumed an expertise for Player B here that he might not have. There are some players that might call, but against a reasonable player in B's position, beware. I have also seen a player in Player C's position bluff, folding Player B, and thereby handing the pot over to Player A, whose hand was inferior to Player B's. This usually brings on a five-minute brouhaha, raising questions about Player C's antecedents, and about C's and A's integrity.

The important lesson to be learned is not to get into a pot with a first-round four flush if one of your opponents already in the pot is short of chips. In this particular example, Player A was all in, but if he had only a few chips left after openers, the reasoning and results would still be much the same.

This situation seems to contradict the optimal strategy outlined in the book. It does not. Before we assumed that all the players had plenty of chips, but when some players are short of chips, new strategies come into play. This seemingly chaotic situation is actually easier and more rational than the examples given in earlier chapters; just beware the lack of a bluff possibility.

Problem 2: In a six-handed, pot-limit, Jacks-or-better game with a $10 ante, you are Player B. Your hand before the draw: 4S, 5S, 6S, 8S, KC. Your hand after the draw: 4S, 5S, 6S, 8S, 10S. Player A comes out of the second round with a $30 bet.

Player	A	B
Position	6	3
First-round betting	—	Pass
	Open $10	Call $10
Cards drawn	Three	One
Second-round betting	Bet $30	?

Player A has drawn three cards and then bet into your flush, what is your play?

Answer: In Problem 2 we take up a question left unanswered in chapter 3: What is the correct strategy for Player B, a first-round four flusher, when the opener deviates from his optimal strategy and comes out on the second round with a bet? To pass would be not only the correct strategy for the opener but plain common sense.

Before the draw, your hand was a four-straight flush, certainly a promising calling hand. After the draw your hand improved to a flush, but unfortunately you missed your straight flush.

It could be argued that Player B is not automatically tagged as a four flusher; some cautious players will pass two pair in a six-handed game when sitting in Position 3. It could also be argued that Player A made three Aces and reasoned that since he would call a bet by Player B, he might as well initiate the bet himself. This is a poor argument because, in this situation, trips is merely a bluff-catching hand. By betting the hand, Player B is not given the chance to bluff.

As Player B, you should be very suspicious of a full house in the offing and suspect that the opener is setting you up for the kill, trying to tempt a raise out of you when you have made your flush, so that he may reraise. However, a flush is too high a hand not to call the opener. Obviously, you should not fold the hand without more evidence of power from the opener.

Proper Play: At a pot-limit game, Player B should only call the opener's bet with his flush but not raise.

If the game is a strict-limit game, or if A is a weak player, you might have a raise, but don't get greedy in a pot-limit game when a player "seems" to have made such an obvious blunder.

Problem 3: In a seven-handed, $20-limit, Jacks-or-better game with a $10 ante, you are Player A. Your hand before the draw: A, A, 4, 8, 9. Your hand after the draw: A, A, A, 2, 9.

Player	A	B	C	D
Position	5	6	7	4
First-round betting	—	—	—	Pass
	Open $10	Call $10	Call $10	Call $10
Cards drawn	Three	Three	One	One
Second-round betting	Pass	Pass	Bet $20	Call $20
	?			

You, Player A, have made three Aces, what action do you take after Player C has bet and D has called?

Answer: The pot contains $90, and it will only cost you $20 to call. As tempting as the pot may be, you should fold. The only possible hand that would justify D's action is a first-round four flush or a four straight that improves to a flush or straight on the second round. (Remember that D passes in Position 4 in a seven-handed game.) Player C may have two pair, a bust, or possibly a big hand. You would have called C's bet if it were not for D. But once D has called, you have no reason to be anywhere near the pot with three Aces, no matter how favorable the odds.

Proper Play: Player A should fold.

Problem 4: In an eight-handed, $20-limit, Jacks-or-better game with a $10 ante, you are Player A. Your hand before the draw: K, K, 2, 2, 7.

Player	A	B	C	D
Position	3	5	7	1
First-round betting	—	—	—	Pass
	Open $10	Call $10	Call $10, raise $20	Call $30
	?			

There is more information in this example. After Player C raised the pot, the player in Position 8 folded, and then Player D, in Position 1, called and threw in $10. He is then reminded that the pot had been raised and to call he must put in $30 not $10. Player D then corrects his call to $30. What do you, Player A, do when the betting comes to you as the opener?

Answer: If D had not come in the pot, you might have

called the raise with Kings-up. Perhaps C is making a bluff raise, and you might possibly (but not probably) have the best hand even if C were not bluffing. However, after D entered the pot and called a raised pot, you should fold with Kings-up. You are beaten and the $90 pot is not giving you enough odds for going for a full house.

Don't be mislead by D's feigned ignorance of the raise— his pretending that he doesn't have a raising hand, but merely a calling hand. Player D's tactic is especially profitable in a limit game where the profit often comes from doing a volume business. Here D is trying to keep both you and Player B in the pot with his hustling tactics. If D reraises he would probably drive both you and Player B out of the pot. Player D's tactic is slightly shoddy but not illegal. The warning signal, of course, is that a first-rate player would certainly be aware of a raise.

Proper Play: Player A should fold.

Problem 5: In a six-handed, $10 and $20 limit, Jacks-or-better game with a $10 ante, you are Player A. Your hand before the draw: A, A, 10, 10, 8. Your hand after the draw: A, A, 10, 10, 9.

Player	A	B
Position	2	3
First-round betting	Open $10	Call $10
Cards drawn	1	Pat!
Second-round betting	Pass	Bet $20
	?	

Should you, Player A, call the $20 bet by Player B?

Answer: You opened with a relatively strong hand, Aces-up. Player B, immediately to your left, called and no other callers came along. You drew one card and B stands pat!

The obvious inference is that B has a straight or better and that he did not raise, hoping not to scare away more callers. By this reasoning you should drop the hand. But what else could B be up to?

Suppose B had two small pair when you opened. Player B had a calling hand according to his optimal strategy. Now, when you drew one card, B figured you had at least two pair and, in all likelihood, had his miserable two small pair beat —at least in the first round. Player B knows that his chances of improvement are slight, 1 in 12. So B stands pat and bets out on the second round, hoping to scare you out of the pot.

Both are good explanations of what an expert player might do. The only way to learn for sure what he is up to is to call. However, as we discussed in chapter 3, your optimal strategy is not to call all the time. Because B bets $20 to win $30, you should call with the top three-fifths or 60 percent of your top hands. Your Aces-up are well within the top three-fifths of your hands on the second round when you draw one card.

Proper Play: Player A should call Player B's $20 bet.

In this book, we have advised you to raise in a six-handed game whenever you have a raising hand. But many players do not follow this strategy. Obviously you cannot count on your opponents to follow the same strategy that you do. Usually when the situation described in Problem 4 arises, it is a sucker play to try to bluff you out of the pot.

Problem 6: In an eight-handed, pot-limit, Jacks-or-better game with a $10 ante, you are Player C. Your hand before the draw: 4, 4, 4, 8, 9.

Player	A	B	C
Position	1	2	6
First-round betting	Open $10	Call $10	?

What action should you, Player C, take with your trip 4s?

Answer: Everyone between you and Player B has folded, and the betting has now come to you. At this point you will notice a decided change in the rhythm. Opening under the gun in an eight-handed game takes a strong hand. You should therefore suspect that Player A has a very big hand and has decided not to sandbag. You should also be wary of Player B's having a big hand. He may prefer to call rather than to raise, trying to collect further first-round bets, or he may be hoping for a raise from some player to his left. We may be wrong about whether A or B is the player with the big hand, but it is almost certain that one of them has a big hand.

However, your trip 4s, which is ordinarily a raising hand, is too strong simply to throw away. While you should not be too optimistic about winning the pot, you are getting about the right odds for your hand when you call.

Proper Play: Player C should call with his hand but not raise.

Problem 7: In a seven-handed, pot-limit, Jacks-or-better game with a $10 ante, you are Player A. Your hand before the draw: K, K, J, 2, 4. Your hand after the draw: K, K, K, 7, 8.

Player	A	B	C
Position	6	8	5
First-round betting	—	—	Pass
	Open $10	Call $10	Call $10
Cards drawn	3	3	1
Second-round betting	Pass	Pass	Bet $40
	?		

178

Player	A	B	C	D	E
Position	4	5	6	7	8
First-round betting	Open $10	Call $10	Call $10	Call $10	Call $10
Cards drawn	Pat	One	Three	One	One
Second-round betting	Pass				

What action should you, Player A, take if B bets? C bets? D bets? E bets?

Answer: For the moment you are overjoyed at the number of calls your fullhouse has netted you on the first round; the pot now contains $60. At the beginning of the second round you have passed in full view of the many one-card draws and callers. You would certainly not come out betting with a straight, so your full house has "cover." You have a powerful hand, and there is no question that you would call a $20 bet by any of the other players, but the question is which of the players will you raise.

If either Player D or E is the first to bet, then you should definitely raise. If either D or E can bet into a pat hand, the odds are that he has a flush. If C comes out with a bet, you should certainly not raise. The only hand, other than a bluff, that would justify a bet by C is a full house, and if C has a full house it will probably be a higher one than yours. (Player C drew three cards.)

Your greatest problem arises if B makes a bet. Player B drew one card, and on the first round he was the first caller. It is more likely that he started out on the first round with two pair than with a four flush. If B started out with two pair and filled up, it is a good chance that you are beaten.

Proper Play: Player A should call B or C but not raise. Player A should raise any bet from D or E.

181

Problem 10: In a seven-handed, pot-limit, Jacks-or-better game with a $10 ante, you are Player B. Your hand before the draw: A, A, K, K, 5. Your hand after the draw: A, A, A, K, K.

Player	A	B	C	D
Position	4	5	2	3
First-Round	—	—	Pass	Pass
	Open $10	Call $10	Call $10	Call $10
Cards drawn	2	1	1	1
Second-Round	Pass	Pass	Bet $50	Fold
	Call $50, raise $150	?		

After C bets and A raises, what action do you, Player B, take with your full house?

Answer: On the first round you hold Aces-up and call the opener. Your hand improves in the draw to an Ace-high full house. On the second round you check, trying to tempt the two four flushes on your left to bet.

Your analysis of the action should be along the following lines: From the first-round action you strongly suspect that both Players C and D backed into the pot with four flushes. When C bets, you should play him for a flush, unless he is bluffing. Player A drew two cards and A raised the pot on the second round, signifying at least a full house, again if A is not bluff raising.

Look at A's actions a bit closer. On the first round you should play A for trips for two reasons. First, there is no reason for A not to draw down to his hand, especially after two four flushes backed in. Remember, that C and D drew before A drew. Second, in A's position the minimal opening hand is a pair of Kings. Thus, your possession of three Aces and two Kings makes it unlikely that A had only a pair on the first round.

If A started with trips, drew two cards, and improved to at least a full house, there is a 41 percent chance that A has four of a kind. That is, in the 2 out of 5 times when A improves to a full house or better by drawing two cards to trips, he winds up with four of a kind.

Certainly B has a good call with Aces-full, but for B to swing out with a $250 raise would be very foolish, facing a two-out-of-five chance of four of a kind ready to swing back with a $750 re-re-raise. There might be some arguments for a raise if A has very little money left, but even then you should just call, on the hope that C might also call. Player C has a fairly hopeless call with a flush, but there is a possibility that C might have a full house, and if not, at least give C a chance to make a mistake by calling with a flush.

Proper Play: Player B should only call the $200 bet. Player B should not reraise.

Problem 11: In a seven-handed, pot-limit, Jacks-or-better game with a $10 ante, you are Player B. Your hand before the draw: Q, Q, 3, 3, 2. Your hand after the draw: Q, Q, 3, 3, 3.

Player	A	B	C	D
Position	7	2	4	5
First-Round	—	Pass	Pass	Pass
	Open $10	Call $10	Call $10	Call $10
Cards drawn	One	One	One	One
Second-Round	Pass	Pass	Pass	Bet $50
	Call $50, raise $150	?		

What action do you, Player B, take with your full house after D has raised?

Answer: As the second man in a seven-man game your proper play is to pass Queens-up, backing in when the pot is opened. Once C and D back in and draw one card, you should play them both for four flushes. Thus, your proper play on the second round at pot limit is to pass automatically, and this you have done. Now D has bet and the opener, after having drawn one card, raises.

The question you must answer is, does your hand give you good enough odds to call a $300 pot for $200? To justify a call, you should have at least a two-out-of-five chance of beating Player A.

Neither Player C nor D is a threat to you. When A raises D, Player A is claiming at least a full house, but he may be bluffing. If A is playing correctly, one-third of A's raises are bluffs. If A is not bluffing, Player B has about a one-in-eleven chance of having the best hand. (This would definitely put A on a full house as there is no point in false carding against two four flushes.) There are 13 different full houses, but Player B's possession of the three 3s and two Queens leaves only eleven. Player B will have the best hand only if A has Deuces-full, therefore B has only a one-in-eleven chance of coming out a winner if A is not bluffing. These odds do not quite justify B's calling A.

However, there is a stronger reason for B not to call: On the first round B had a Deuce, lowering by three-fourths the chances that A has Deuces-full. The fact that B saw a deuce makes the odds now quite a bit out of line for a call. It is not expected that a player could sit down and quickly compute the odds of having the best hand in B's position, but a good player would certainly take into account his having the Deuce on the first round, pretty much indicating defeat.

Proper Play: Player B should fold.

There is an interesting psychological trap here. This full house may be the best hand you will hold all evening. You will feel ridiculous if Player A is bluffing. Also, if Player A is not bluffing and you call, all the players will sympathize with your "bad luck" in having your full house beaten by a higher full house. But these are the rationalizations of a "loser." Poker should be played to maximize money, not ego.

This situation arises fairly often, and the correct play for B is to call A's raise with 4s-full or better. Of course, the side cards are important. Call with 4s-full if the side pair are 5s or better, but not if the side pair are Deuces or 3s. In our example A raised the size of the pot, but the answer is the same if A had only raised any amount over one-half of the pot.

INDEX

187

Index